RESCUE 007

4691-SCHL

RESCUE 007

*The Untold Story of
KAL 007 and Its Survivors*

Bert Schlossberg

To order additional copies of this book, contact:
Xlibris Corporation
1-888-7-XLIBRIS
www.Xlibris.com
Orders@Xlibris.com

CONTENTS

DEDICATED TO EXIE,
MY BELOVED WIFE,
WHO HAS BEEN IN MY HEART AND MIND
THROUGHOUT THE WRITING OF THIS BOOK.

PREFACE

As I delved into the matter of my father-in-law's disappearance along with the other 268 passengers and crew of the ill-fated Korean Airlines flight 007 of September 1, 1983, the terms of the central enigma became clear.

If, as Marshal Nicolay Ogarkov, U.S.S.R. Chief of General Staff, had stated, nine days after the fact, and as we all knew from day one, that the jet the Russians had shot down was a civilian passenger liner rather than a military plane, then there ought to have been certainly more than 260 people found at the site, dead or alive, either in the water or on the water (in boats or rafts) or still in the aircraft—or they ought to have been under the water dead.

If not a single person, dead or alive, was found floating on the surface of the water at the arrival of Soviet vessels just 27 minutes after KAL 007 had "crashed"—as Admiral Vladimir Vasilyevich Siderov, the commander of the Soviet Pacific Fleet and commander of KAL 007's Soviet salvage operation had stated, then passengers and crew ought to have been trapped in the sinking aircraft and were now confined in some segment of their watery tomb.

And if there were no bodies found under water within the wreckage of the jumbo jet, as stated publicly eight years after the fact (when the communist grip and gags were loosening) by amazed and perplexed Russian civilian divers ordered down by the Soviet authorities, then that, indeed, constituted an enormous mystery – one to be solved.

Where were flight 007's passengers and crew?

*   *   *

I should not have been the one to write this book—there are many others more gifted than I. Yet, in an unplanned and unexpected way, the strange confluence of events and circumstances brought me forth, and, as it seemed, only me, to pen these events. It would be literally "to pen", as I know neither the computer arts nor even simple typing—though, wondrously, I had been a university teacher. The work of transferring what was in my mind, through my pen point, to the form of what you will read, has been effected by the typing skills of my good wife, Exie, and my capable daughters, Charisma and Judith, and by the computer expertise of Old Friend and Constant Support, the Rev. Reuben G. Torrey.

The strange confluence of events and circumstances that has enabled me to write this book has been, firstly, my being married to a daughter of Alfredo Cruz who occupied a seat in row forty of the ill-fated flight. Through Exie's pain and through her faith, I could do no other than pursue this to the end. She has given me what I needed to persevere—love, understanding, encouragement, and time.

Secondly, I am a text man. My previous training and enjoyment in dealing with a single topic (the Biblical Story) through the kaleidoscopic prisms of four pertinent languages (Hebrew, Greek, Aramaic, and Syriac) have enabled me to tell "the KAL 007 Story" bringing to bear and making into one whole the many and variegated, relevant, and hitherto unculled and unassembled sources, in order to experience, if only vicariously, what it was like to have been shot down and to be rescued.

The one great obstacle to credibility in the whole endeavor is this—the entire scenario we will experience as we go through this book:

- The irritation of Major Osipovich at missing his best shot as Capt. Chun Byung-In suddenly noses the jumbo jet up for a steep climb, brought to us via U.S. National Security Agency intercepts

- The tension-filled but effectively purposeful interchanges and action of Capt. Chun and his co-pilot in KAL 007's cockpit right after the missile strike—brought to us via the Cockpit Voice Recorder tapes

- The dismay and confusion, and subordinate-directed haranguing of General Kornukov as he becomes aware that KAL 007 not only has survived the attack but that it is quite maneuverable

- The ineptitude yet, paradoxically, commanding decisiveness of General Strogov as he orders civilian ships and the KGB patrol boats to converge on Moneron Island to effect the rescue brought to us via real-time ground-to-ground Russian High Command communiqués

All this, and more, may create in us by the realism, by the excitement, the sense and suspicion that all is staged. That it is fiction. That it is a movie script for someone of the caliber of, say, Steven Spielberg—for a Schindler's List or Saving Private Ryan level of cinematic experience. But it is not. It all happened in real life and it is documented.

To continue mentioning the people that have helped in the producing of this book, of special note are Abraham and Eleanora Shifrin. The Shifrins are the real investigators and prime movers of the KAL 007 incident. Without them, very little, if anything, would have come to light about the fact and circumstances of the rescue. You will hear much about, and much from, them in this book.

And then there are two other Schlossbergs I need mention—my brother Herb and his son, Steven. Herb helped me by setting my perspective straight and honoring me by his comments and suggestions (you see, I am a not so young, yet still younger brother). I once requested of Herb, presently an author and, at one time, a financial consultant, to give me some financial advice. He did. He told me to get a job! More pertinently, but in a similar vein, in response to my question, prior to the completion of the revision of this book, if he were convinced by it, he said, "You have a good case. But to be convinced, I need to hear the rebuttals." It is this sort of merciless mercy and rigidity that has been very helpful to me.

The other Schlossberg, my nephew Steve, also an author, has the knack of getting inside one's head and one's feelings and expressing it all in sheer writ. He has done this in the writing of the Introduction. It is his work.

And then there are the pictures, these, too, have helped me. These are pictures from *Time*, *People*, and *Life* magazines—pictures of faces full of happiness and hope. These are the victims. And pictures of the victims' families at the time of their bereavement and pain—the fathers and mothers, the sons and daughters, the little children, the wives and the husbands, the brothers and the sisters; these, too, have helped me. I can't look long at the photos of the victims. I know they are still alive.

Finally, I want to express gratitude to God for seeing this through and effecting for us all, Rescue and Homecoming.

"For God shall bring every work into judgment, with every secret thing, whether it be good or whether it be evil." Ecclesiastes 12:14.

Bert Schlossberg
December 25, 2000
Jerusalem

INTRODUCTION

On an oily August evening in New York City, Dr. Larry McDonald boarded a Korean Airlines Boeing 747. A forty-eight year old urologist, McDonald was the father of five. He was also a Democratic congressman from Georgia, and chairman of the right-wing John Birch Society.

He was now on his way to Seoul, South Korea, to attend the anniversary celebration of the Mutual Defense Treaty between the United States and the Republic of Korea. It was 1983. Ronald Reagan was in his first presidential term, Yuri Andropov was the Soviet Premier, and the whole world seemed cast in the shadow of two superpowers locked in a struggle for its mastery.

Rain poured out of the black skies as the jet departed Kennedy Airport, but so uneventful was the first leg of the flight that McDonald slept through the layover in Anchorage, Alaska, seven hours later. By then it was a new day, August 31.

At 4:00 a.m. KAL 007 departed Anchorage with a new crew. The pilot in command was now Chun Byung-In. The same age as his passenger McDonald, Chun was a former colonel in the Korean Air Force, a black belt in Tae Kwon Do, and a man so meticulously obsessive about details that, according to his wife, if a picture on a wall was out of place by so much as a nail's width, he would rehang it.

Within ten minutes of its Anchorage departure, however, Captain Chun's plane was drifting disastrously off course.

Between the coasts of Alaska and Japan there are five 50 mile-wide air corridors, the NOPAC (North Pacific Composite) routes, the northernmost of which is called Romeo 20. This was the flight path to which KAL 007 had been assigned. Inexplicably, Captain Chun never found it. Approximately ten minutes after takeoff, the jumbo jet began to deviate to the west. Twenty minutes after takeoff, civilian radar at Kenai, Alaska, tracked KAL 007 at more than a six mile deviation and 50 minutes after takeoff, military radar at King's Salmon, Alaska, tracked KAL 007 at a full 12 miles north of its plotted course. [1] One after another, KAL007 plunged through its checkpoints, ever increasing its deviation—60 nautical miles off course at waypoint NABIE, 100 nautical miles off course at waypoint NUKKS, and 160 nautical miles off course at waypoint NEEVA[2]— until, three and a half hours after takeoff, it entered Russian territory just north of the port city of Petropavslovsk on the Kamchatka Peninsula. Home to the Far East Fleet Inter-Continental Ballistic Nuclear Submarine Base (thirty ballistic missile and ninety attack submarines) as well as several military airfields, Petropavslovsk was bristling with weaponry.

August 31/September 1, 1983, was the worst possible night for KAL 007 to "bump the buffer" for a complexity of reasons—each of them ominous. It was but a few short hours before the test firing of the SS-25, an illegal mobile Inter-Continental Ballistic Missile (ICBM).[3] The SS-25 was to be launched from Plesetsk, the launch site in northwest Russia, which was used for test firing solid fuel

---

[1] ICAO 1983 report, p. 5. For a detailed account of KAL 007's flight, and the mystery surrounding its deviation from its flight plan, see Appendix D.

[2] ICAO report 1993, p. 45, sect. 2.8.1.

[3] The SS-25 was in violation of the SALT II agreements on three counts:

- It was a new kind of ICBM (the first mobile ICBM ever launched).
- Its telemetry was encoded and encrypted. When a test ICBM re-entry vehicle approaches its target, it emits vital data relating to its size, trajectory, throw-weight, and accuracy by means of coded (symbolized) and encrypted (scrambled) electronic bursts, which are then decoded and decrypted by Soviet on-ground intelligence-gathering stations.
- The missile as a whole was too large for its re-entry vehicle (dummy warhead), raising the suspicion that the missile was being developed for new and more advanced warheads than allowable.

propellant ICBMs—24 minutes later to land in the Klyuchi target area on the Kamchatka Peninsula.[4]

As Soviet aerial "jammers" under Maskirovka[5] were sent aloft to prevent United States intelligence from obtaining the SS-25's telemetry data, an RC-135 Boeing 707 reconnaissance plane was "lazy eighting" off the Kamchatka peninsula coast, electronically "sucking in" emissions. The Soviets would also contend that KAL 007's entire flight—from the time prior to its entry into Soviet airspace off Kamchatka, until it was shot down—dovetailed with three passes of a United States Ferret-D intelligence-gathering satellite, which would have therefore been apprised of KAL 007's progress into airspace over super-sensitive Soviet military installations.

Well within range of United States Air Force radar stations at Cape Newenham and Cape Romanzoff in Alaska, KAL 007 had veered directly toward Kamchatka. These radar stations were required to warn the straying aircraft on emergency frequency, as well as other pertinent Air Traffic Control Centers so that they too could attempt to warn the straying aircraft.

But that night KAL 007 plunged through the Russian 200 kilometer buffer zone, then the 100 kilometer Air Defense Zone, and then it was over Soviet territory with no one to stop it.

On board the jumbo jet all was as usual. 90 minutes after takeoff, according to KAL practice, the stewardesses would have donned their "chima" and "chogori"—their long Korean dresses and exotic blouses. Sandwiches and soft drinks were served to economy class passengers, while zucchini au gratin and Chicken Florentine were served in the first class compartment. Lights were then dimmed and a feature film shown. Many of the passengers were stretched across two or three seats, dozing, as the plane was only three-quarters full.

KAL 007 crossed the Kamchatka Peninsula, and while over the international waters of the Sea of Okhotsk nearing the coast of Sakhalin, a "welcome" was being frantically prepared for it 33 thousand feet below—documented by the transcripts of the Russian mili-

---

[4] Liquid propellant ICBMs were launched from Tyuratam in southwest Russia.

[5] The Strategic Deception Department, charged with hiding Salt 2 violations from United States intelligence.

tary ground-to-ground communications submitted by the Russian Federation and appended to the 1993 ICAO report.

General Kornukov:[6] (6:13)[7]
"Chaika."[8]

Titovnin:[9]
Yes, sir. He[10] sees [*it*] on the radar screen, he sees [*it*] on the screen. He has locked on, he is locked on, he is locked on.

Kornukov:
No answer, Roger. Be ready to fire, the target is 45-50 kilometers from the State border.[11] Officer in charge of the command post, please, for report.

Titovnin:
Hello.

---

[6] General Anatoli Kornukov, Commander Sokol Air Force Base (Sakhalin). Kornukov was appointed Russia's new Air Force Commander by Boris Yeltsin on January 22, 1998.

[7] Numbers in parentheses are the times of transmission to the minute or second depending on source of transcript. Numbers to the minute are not repeated until the minute changes.

[8] Call sign for Far East Military District Air Force.

[9] Flight Controller for Major Osipovich—Combat Control Center of Fighter Division.

[10] Major Gennadie Osipovich, flying a Sukhoi 15 Flagon interceptor—call sign 805. The Sukhoi SU—15TM "Flagon—F" designed in 1971, entered service in 1975 and was used by the PVO (Soviet Home Defense Units) in the Far East through the mid 1990s until it was replaced by the MiG 31, "Foxhound," and the Sukhoi 21 "Flanker." The Sukhoi Flagon, flown by Major Osipovich, was generally armed with two AA—3 "Anab" medium range air-to-air missiles.

[11] Apparently, the Soviets were prepared to fire while KAL 007 was in international air space. It had previously been flying over Russian territory.

Kornukov:

Kornukov, please put Kamenski on the line . . . General Kornukov, put General Kamenski[12] on.

General Kamenski:

Kamenski here.

Kornukov: (6:14)

Comrade General, Kornukov, good morning. I am reporting the situation. Target 60-65[13] is over Terpenie Bay[14] tracking 240, 30 km from the State Border, the fighter from Sokol is 6 km away. Locked on, orders were given to arm weapons. The target is not responding, to identify, he cannot identify it visually because it is still dark, but he is still locked on.

Kamenski:

We must find out, maybe it is some civilian craft or God knows who.

Kornukov:

What civilian? [It] has flown over Kamchatka! It [came] from the ocean without identification. I am giving the order to attack if it crosses the State border.

Kamenski:

Go ahead now, I order. . . ?

And at another location—Smirnykh Air Force Base in central Sakhalin . . .

---

[12] Commander, Far East Military District Air Force.

[13] Call sign for KAL 007 "intruder."

[14] Terpenie Bay is on the east coast of Sakhalin Island. KAL 007 had thus successfully traversed Kamchatka, and crossing the Sea of Okhotsk, it was about to enter Sakhalin's air space.

Lt. Col. Novoseletski:[15] **(6:12)**
Does he see it on the radar or not?

Titovnin: (6:13)
He sees it on the screen, he sees it on the screen. He is locked on.

Novoseletski:
He is locked on.

Titovnin:
Locked on. Well, Roger.

Titovnin: (6:14)
Hello.

Lt. Col. Maistrenko:[16]
Maistrenko!

Titovnin:
Maistrenko Comrade Colonel, that is, Titovnin.

Maistrenko: (6:15)
Yes.

Titovnin:
The commander has given orders that if the border is violated—
destroy [*the target*].

Maistrenko:
. . . may [*be*] a passenger [*aircraft*]. All necessary steps must be taken
to identify it.

Titovnin:
Identification measures are being taken, but the pilot cannot see. It's
dark. Even now it's still dark.

---

[15] Smirnykh Air Base Fighter Division Acting Chief of Staff.

[16] Operations Duty Officer, Combat Control Center of Fighter Division.

Maistrenko:
Well, okay. The task is correct. If there are no lights—it cannot be a passenger [*aircraft*].

Titovnin:
You confirm the task?

Maistrenko:
Eh?

Titovnin:
You confirm the task?

Maistrenko:
Yes.

Titovnin:
Roger.

And at yet another location—with KAL007 already having entered Sakhalin airspace and with only five minutes of flying time before being rocketed . . .

Kornukov: (6:21)
Gerasimenko!

Lt. Col. Gerasimenko:[17]
Gerasimenko here.

Kornukov:
Gerasimenko, cut the horseplay at the command post, what is that noise there? I repeat the combat task: fire the missiles, fire on target 60-65, destroy target 60-65.

---

[17] Acting Commander, 41st Fighter Regiment.

Gerasimenko: (6:22)
Wilco.

Kornukov:
Comply and get Tarasov[18] here.
Take control of the MiG 23 from Smirnykh, call sign 163, call sign
    163, he is behind the target at the moment. Destroy the target!

Gerasimenko:
Task received. Destroy target 60-65 with missile fire, accept control
    of fighter from Smirnykh.

Kornukov:
Carry out the task, destroy [*it*]!

Gerasimenko:
. . . Comrade General . . . Gone to attack position.

Kornukov: (6:24)
Oh, [*obscenities*], how long [*does it take him*] to go to attack position,
    he is already getting out into neutral waters. Engage afterburner
    immediately. Bring in the MiG 23 as well . . . While you are
    wasting time, it will fly right out.
Gerasimenko.

Gerasimenko:
Here.
Kornukov:
So, 23[19] is going behind, his radar sights are engaged, draw yours off
    to the right immediately after the attack. Has he fired or not?

Gerasimenko:
Not yet, not at all.

---

[18] Pilot of Sukhoi SU—15, Flagon, call sign 121, flying in support position to
    Osipovich's Flagon.
[19] MiG 23.

Kornukov:
Why?

Gerasimenko:
He is closing in, going on the attack. 163[20] is coming in, observing both.

Kornukov:
Okay, Roger, understood, so bring in 163 in behind Osipovich to guarantee destruction.

About two hours earlier, the Korean Boeing 747 had been picked up by Soviet radars as it approached the Kamchatka Peninsula. It successfully passed over the peninsula without being located by three pairs of hastily scrambled interceptors. As it crossed the international waters of the Sea of Okhotsk and reentered Soviet airspace as it approached Sakhalin Island, four more Soviet interceptors were scrambled, and now the lead plane, a Sukhoi 15 (Flagon) piloted by Major Osipovich, received orders to destroy the intruder. Kornukov, viewing the airliner from his radar position, has decided on the timing of the destruct order.

At 6:21 a.m., Pilot Chun and his copilot appear relaxed and totally oblivious to the Flagon stalking them. This can be seen by their intermittent yawns and chit-chat:

"I have heard that there is currency exchange at our airport."

"In the airport currency exchange? What kind of money?"

"Dollars to Korean money."

"That is in the Domestic building too."[21]

---

[20] Call sign for the MiG 23.

[21] "Report of the Completion of the Fact Finding Investigation regarding the shoot down of the Korean Air Line Boeing 747 (Flight KE007) on 31 August 1983, United Nations Security Council—139th session." Information paper no. 1, CVR Transcript, p. 10. This type of banter is the prime reason that the International Civil Aviation Organization concluded that "there was no evidence...to indicate that the flight crew of KE007 was, at any time, aware of the flight's deviation from its planned route." ICAO Report 1993, p. 2.

Captain Chun had six minutes earlier, at 6:15, requested permission from the Tokyo controller to ascend from 33,000 to 35,000 feet. That request was granted one minute earlier, at 6:20, and now at 6:21, KAL 007 was in its three minute climb. And, at the same moment—6:21—General Kornukov has made his decision: the intruder must now be destroyed.

Kornukov: (6:21)
Gerasimenko, cut the horseplay at the command post, what is that noise there? I repeat the combat task: fire the missiles, fire on target 60-65 destroy target 60-65.

Gerasimenko: (6:22)
Wilco.

Kornukov:
Comply and get Tarasov here.
Take control of the MiG 23 from Smirnykh, call sign 163, call sign 163, he is behind the target at the moment. Destroy the target!

Gerasimenko:
Task received. Destroy target 60-65 with missile fire, accept control of fighter from Smirnykh.

Kornukov:
Carry out the task, destroy [*it*]![22]

But Flight 007 was to get a brief reprieve. As the jumbo jet climbed, its speed decreased, engine power being diverted from velocity to lift, and Osipovich's Sukhoi 15 quickly overtook and was soon abreast of the passenger plane. Major Osipovich showed irritation as he communicated with his flight controller, Titovnin.

Osipovich: (6:22:02)
The target is decreasing speed.

---
[22] ibid., p. 129.

Osipovich: (6:22:17)
I am going around it. I'm already moving in front of the target.

Titovnin:[23]
Increase speed, 805 [*call sign of Osipovich's Sukhoi*].

Osipovich: (6:22:23)
I have increased speed.

Titovnin:
Has the target increased speed, yes?

Osipovich: (6:22:29)
No, it is decreasing speed.

Titovnin:
805, open fire on target.

Osipovich: (6:22:42)
It should have been earlier. How can I chase it? I'm already abeam of
    the target.

Titovnin:
Roger, if possible, take up a position for attack.

Osipovich: (6:22:55)
Now I have to fall back a bit from the target.[24]

Osipovich's irritation with his controller reflects the fact that, in
contrast with the freedom of initiative given to an American pilot in
combat, a Soviet pilot must be "vectored" and commanded for almost
every move he makes.

---

[23] Titovnin's replies to Osipovich are recorded on a separate transcript with a "min-
    utes" indicator but no "seconds" indicator. They are nonetheless easily corre-
    lated with Osipovich's transmissions.

[24] ibid., pp. 69, 70.

KAL 007 leveled off at 6:23 at 35,000 feet. Now it would have only 3 minutes of flying time before Osipovich's "Anab" medium range air-to-air missile would come streaking toward it from the rear. And, it was now General Kornukov's turn to exhibit irritation and concern. From his communication to Gerasimenko, it is clear that KAL 007 was shot down by the Soviets not because it posed a threat to them, but because it was escaping.

Kornukov:
Oh, [*obscenities*] how long does it take him to get into attack position, he is already getting out into neutral waters. Engage afterburner immediately. Bring in the MiG 23 as well . . . While you are wasting time it will fly right out.[25]

With back-up from the MiG 23 (call sign 123), and at a distance of eight kilometers, Major Osipovich executes what he believes will be the destruction of KAL 007 (he has distanced himself from the target so that his interceptor will not be struck by fragments of the exploding passenger plane).

Titovnin:
805, try to destroy the target with cannons.

Osipovich: (6:22:37)
I am dropping back. Now I will try a rocket.

Titovnin:
Roger.

MiG 23 (163): (6:23:49)
Twelve kilometers to the target. I see both [*the Soviet interceptor pi-loted by Osipovich and KAL 007*].

---

[25] ibid., p. 130.

Titovnin:
805, approach target and destroy target.

Osipovich: (6:24:22)
Roger, I am in lock-on.

Titovnin:
805, are you closing on the target?

Osipovich: (6:25:11)
I am closing on the target, am in lock-on. Distance to target is eight
kilometers.

Titovnin:
Afterburner.

Titovnin:
AFTERBURNER, 805!

Osipovich: (6:25:16)
I have already switched it on.

Titovnin:
Launch!

Osipovich: (6:26:20)
I have executed the launch.

Osipovich: (6:26:22)
The target is destroyed.

Titovnin:
Break off attack to the right, heading 360. *[due North]*

Osipovich: (6:26:27)
I am breaking off attack.[26] [27]

---

[26] ibid., pp. 71, 72.

[27] The above ground-to-air, air-to-ground communications between Osipovich and Titovnin have been supplied by the Soviets (Titovnin) and by U.S. National Security Agency sourced intercepts. The tapes of Osipovich to ground controller were played by the US, much to the chagrin of the Russian delegates to the UN Security Council right after the attack. The first time an NSA intercept of an aerial attack against a U.S. plane was made public was of the attack on Sept. 2, 1958. The target was an EC-130 ELINT (Electronic Intelligence) aircraft of the National Security Agency piloted by Air Force Captain Rudy J. Swiestra:

"There's a hit.

The target is banking.

It is going to the fence. . .

Open fire

218, are you attacking?

Yes, yes, I . . .

The target is burning

The tail assembly is falling off the target.

Look!

Oh?

Look at him. He will not get away. He is already falling.

Yes, he is falling. I will finish him off on the run.

The target has lost control. It is going down.

Now the target will fall.

82, a little to the right.

The target has turned over.

The target is falling . . .

Form up . . .

82, I see, I am watching the target. I see.

Aha, you see, it is falling.

Yes . . . form up, go home."

*   *   *

Larry McDonald was the only celebrity aboard KAL 007 that morn-ing, but he was not the only passenger. All told, there were 269 people aboard, including a crew of 23. Among them was Edith Cruz, a 23-year-old medical technologist from Chattanooga, Tennessee, en route to the Philippines to attend her grandmother's funeral. She was trav-eling with her uncle Alfredo, a handsome, 56 year old grandfather with a full head of jet-black hair crowning his proud Asian face. An accountant by trade, he was in many ways a man of detail and preci-sion, a meticulous dresser who for some reason chose that day to wear a white Gloria Vanderbilt shirt he had bought the week before for his daughter Exie. This was "Tay" as we called him, "Dad" in Tagalog.

Exie had begged him not to go. Three months before, she had had a premonition of her father's disappearance. Later she would call it a vision. At the time, though, she had no name for it. She had never had a vision before. While trying to take a nap in her parents' bed-room, she saw a beautiful wreath of flowers being delivered to her parents' living room. She was not sleeping; her eyes were open. Yet, addressing the bedroom wall, she saw the living room. She saw the sun pouring through her parents' living room window and falling upon the great wreath of funeral flowers. Otherwise, the room was empty—there was no casket; there was no body.

"Who are the flowers for?" she asked.

The answer she received—inaudibly, but nonetheless distinctly—was, "For your father."

The vision passed.

And almost as soon as the vision passed, Exie dismissed it. At the time, it seemed meaningless. And by the time of her father's departure three months later, the vision was almost entirely forgotten. Exie's worries now, as she begged him not to go, were much more purely natural. This was to be Tay's first trip back to the Philippines since his emigration to the United States 12 years earlier. Then, Tay had wept, leaving his mother behind. Now he was returning to bury her.

He had a weak heart; now his heart was broken, and Exie worried that the trauma of the funeral, compounded by the stress of overseas travel, might finally break his health. She telephoned him the night of his departure and tried to talk him out of going. He dismissed her every plea with a joke, and then at last, after Exie telephoned him a second time, he confided to her why he felt he had to go.

"It's the last chance I'll have," he said, "to serve my mother."

This was something against which Exie felt she could not argue. She too had been there 12 years earlier, in the terminal of the Manila airport, amid the bewildering clamor of bodies and voices and noises, speechlessly watching a trail of tears disturb her father's proud face. She was 20 years old then, a business school graduate, but she was in many ways still a young girl, still entirely Filipino, and the prospect of casting herself to the fabled and utterly alien shores of America plunged her heart into a whirlpool of conflicting emotions. But more than any of these vivid daydreams and private anxieties, the sight of her father silently weeping indelibly branded her memory.

Her mother and her youngest sister had been in New York three years already. Tay had lagged in order to secure a more permanent Visa, and to allow Exie to complete her education. Perhaps these years together in Manila galvanized the bond between them. In any case, out of the complex and sometimes riotous relationships of a large Catholic family, Exie and her father discovered a quiet, but ironclad, affinity for each other. Evidently Tay had shared a similar bond with his mother. And even I, who three years later married Exie in New York, immediately perceived the bond between them.

Jewish, divorced, non-Roman Catholic, non-Filipino and 13 years Exie's senior, I should have irritated Tay's every prejudice and jealousy. Perhaps I did. But if I did, he masterfully concealed his misgivings. More than that, he received me into his family with warmth, and thereafter treated me with gentle kindness and boundless generosity. He was not an outgoing man; he was quiet with his family, and in larger social gatherings he clung, according to Filipino custom, to the segregated circle of adult men. But apart from the society of adults, he loved to play with his grandchildren. He was an accomplished gardener. And even I, a man on whom subtle signals are sometimes lost, could sense the quiet sympathy that joined him to his daughter Exie.

Exie would later say that in her, Tay discovered someone in whom he could confide, and in her father, Exie had someone who could be trusted to read her silent thoughts, and who knew better than anyone else how to comfort and encourage her. Doubtless this was so, but this does not begin to describe what I observed. What I remember best is this: on Sunday afternoons in New Rochelle, as Exie worked about her parents' house, she would quietly begin to sing songs from her youth. From another room, her father, who himself had a gifted voice, would join her with a merry whistle, harmonic and true. The old house would fill with the music of two hearts caroling like songbirds. It was at such moments that I felt not only that I was seeing the true affinity between father and daughter, but that I was glimpsing the bared soul of my circumspect father-in-law, dancing.

*   *   *

On the evening of August 31, Exie's sister Teresa telephoned us in Connecticut and told us that Tay's plane had been reported missing. Dread plunged through our house. A heavy silence fell over us. We turned on the television and watched reporters repeat the same headline—*Airliner lost!*— urgently, sensationally, but inconclusively. At one point, the plane was rumored to have made a successful emergency landing on the Sakhalin Island, in the Sea of Japan. Beneath the pall of dread, hope would stir in our hearts, then fade, then stir once more. We prayed. We waited. We could not sleep.

At three o'clock the following morning, Teresa called once more. On television, she said, Secretary of State George Schultz was announcing that KAL 007 had been shot down by two Soviet missiles, and there were no survivors.

Instantaneously, the pall of dread disappeared, and with it, all hope. Exie left the bedroom. I heard her exit the kitchen door and enter the back yard. Then I heard her scream.

I thought at first that she would quit when she reached the end of her first breath. I was still digesting the Secretary of State's announcement, repeating it to myself, probing it in my mind, incredulously. Perhaps I was waiting for the news to change, as it had the night before.

Meanwhile, Exie continued screaming. She screamed for her father, *Tay*. She reached the end of her first breath, and then she drew another and screamed again. In Bolton, Connecticut, that night the air was warm and clear, the sky a pinpricked canopy of winking stars. Exie shattered it with her voice. I did not recognize her voice. I had never before heard her scream. She had never before tasted death.

She continued so until well after dawn broke. I comforted her as best I could but nothing seemed to help. When she finally came inside I could see that she was changed. Grief had remade her. Beneath the beautiful shape of her face something harder than bone described the line of her jaw, and her eyes no longer sparkled. We had three children then—the oldest seven years old, the youngest two—and I had already fed them breakfast. This would be the pattern for the next while.

That morning we drove to the house in New Rochelle, among the last of the family to arrive. Exie immediately bolted up the stairs and shut herself in a bedroom, weeping alone. Our children milled about with their cousins, bewildered. I stood in the living room, somewhat abstracted from the others. I was somewhat abstracted from their grief. Watching the television—watching an endless parade of chattering reporters urgently repeat themselves: Airliner Shot Down! No Survivors!—I began to reserve my emotions. In the tumult of a violent world, it seemed my emotions were the only thing over which I had any control anymore.

Then I saw Exie descending the stairs. Halfway down she stopped. Clutching the banister, she seemed to petrify. She was looking past her parents' living room into the entrance vestibule. The sun was pouring through the window onto a great funeral wreath. There was no casket. There was no body. The vision had become reality.

*　*　*

There would be no body, ever. And that, as the years passed, seemed the enduring indignity. That seemed the final injustice. We attended a series of memorial services—in New York, in Washington, D. C., in South Korea. We accompanied Exie's mother Roberta, a devout woman who as a young girl had endured the Japanese invasion of her village, on a pilgrimage to Jerusalem for the healing of her grief. But the iron jaws of grief are not so easily pried open. Not for Exie's mother, and not for Exie. For days on end she sobbed ceaselessly, and when her tears were utterly exhausted she made noises like those of dry heaving. Her wasted throat choked and brayed. Then, when her tear ducts recovered, she sobbed again.

For months it went on. Anything—the sight of an old knick-knack, the strains of an old melody, or sometimes seemingly nothing at all—would touch off a memory, and she would burst into tears. The ancient Hebrews did not distinguish between body and spirit, and in Exie's grief I saw how completely they are fused indeed. Her sorrow crippled her. Later she said that she felt her grief as a deep chasm in her belly, the bottom of which it seemed she would never reach. For me, her grief was an interminable stretch of time, the end of which would never arrive. Years passed so. In Israel, she began cutting out newspaper photographs of terrorist victims and their families.

There was no body. We felt robbed by this. Unable to bury the body of Tay, we felt unable to heal the trench hacked out of our lives. Phrases like "monstrous injustice," so often uttered by so many victims that the words seem shopworn and dull, suddenly became intensely vivid and, proceeding from our own mouths, charged with meaning. We began to appreciate what the families of MIA soldiers must daily endure, forever.

There was no body. KAL 007 left no bodies at all. For years this was like a canker on our hearts. Then one day it became a curiosity to our minds.

There were no bodies.

Why were there no bodies?

That was the question that launched our family on a bizarre odyssey that would fling us as far afield as the war torn city of Jerusalem. It would sweep us into a grieving field of black umbrellas in Changyang, Korea. It would lead us to clandestine meetings with a former Soviet radar operator and with the Korean CIA. It would bring us into the possession of both sensitive and declassified documents from the American CIA and the U.S. Seventh Fleet. It would transport us, if only vicariously, into the cockpit of a Soviet Sukhoi Flagon interceptor as it launched its rockets, and into the cockpit of the Korean airliner moments before, during and after the rocket detonation. It would plunge us beneath the cold seas off the coast of eastern Russia, and behind the masks of rescue divers crawling over and into the sunken wreckage.

It would lead us finally, reluctantly, to the conclusion that the true fate of KAL 007 and its passengers has never been fully reported.

In all likelihood, the passengers survived, Tay had survived!

This is our story.

Alfredo Cruz with his daughter, Exie

Alfredo Cruz—seated in row 40, Korean Air Lines flight 007

Edith Cruz—seated in row 40, Korean Air Lines flight 007

Author and his wife, Exie

Exie Cruz Schlossberg

CHAPTER 1

The Israel Connection

Holy Land to three faiths, Israel seems to capture the imagination of all who visit it. So it was with me, who in my early twenties spent six months there on a kibbutz. Decades later my memories of Israel seemed to grow only more vivid, my sentiments for the land more intense, and I found myself praying that God would make a way for me to return. Exie later joined me in this hope. After years of prayer and preparation, we finally moved to Jerusalem in 1988, renting a cottage right across the street from the Hyatt Hotel, in a section of the city that had become part of Israel after the 1967 Six Day War. A year later we bought a house in Pisgat Zeev, where we've lived ever since.

We had four children by then. Charisma Joy, Daniel Abraham, Judith Hope and Jonathan David were all not yet teenagers, I was fifty years old (Exie was the glue that held us together), and the challenge of transplanting a Connecticut Yankee family into the harsh, hard soil of the Middle East nearly overwhelmed us. Homesick, we had a new language to learn, a foreign diet, a strange currency, tumultuous politics, unfamiliar customs, and breathtakingly bad driving habits (eleven years later, I have yet to completely acclimate myself to my countrymen's driving habits!). We learned to live in a city of steep hills, skinny streets, abrupt manners, and precious little greenery. We grew familiar with war and rumors of war. We grew accustomed to seeing soldiers on our street corners. Such challenges, of course, do have their satisfactions, as well as their cathartic effects, and among these, for Exie, was the slow scabbing-over of her grief.

Then one afternoon in 1991, a neighbor showed us an article in a Hebrew newspaper announcing a press conference at which a man named

Avraham Shifrin would announce his preliminary findings of the KAL 007 shoot-down. I had never before heard of Shifrin, and the article gave little clue as to what his findings indicated, but seeing "KAL 007" in print again made my stomach turn. Even as old memories were aroused and old curiosity excited, I wished my neighbor had not thought to bring this to our attention. Exie studied the article; I looked at Exie and my heart fell. Her eyes were clear, her face perfectly composed, but I could see the scabs of her grief torn and opened beneath her skin, and yet I knew she would not let this rest.

We could not let this rest. Driven rather more by a sense of compulsion than by any particular hope, we contacted Shifrin, who invited us to meet him at his home, a modest four-bedroom apartment high on a hill in the Ramot section of Jerusalem. He met us at the door with his wife Eleanora, a slender, handsome woman with a face of intelligent kindness. She greeted us as mourners, and conducting us into their small living room, she served us tea.

Her husband, a thick chested man with a full head of white hair, did not waste much time with pleasantries. He was by no means unkind. He was direct. He was a man from whom the best years of his life had been robbed, and he spoke like a man for whom every minute counts.[28]

We noticed immediately that he walked with a limp, but it was only months later that we learned why. It was as a result of war wounds to both legs resulting in the amputation of one, and of Soviet torture requiring him to remain standing in icy water up to his knees in his cell at Lubyanka Central Prison during the bitter winter months. When Avraham was in his usual state of pain and inquiry was made concerning his health, his reply was "Oh, fine." When his pain was almost beyond bearing, he would stoically reply, "My leg hurts." [29]

---

[28] Avraham Shifrin died in Jerusalem on March 5, 1998.

[29] Shifrin's friend, Richard Wurmbrand, Director of Voice of the Martyrs, a mission organization serving those who suffer under Communism, also has trouble with his feet. Beaten on the soles of his feet by the Rumanian Communist interrogators, even now Wurmbrand can hardly walk. His sermons must be preached sitting down.

He was reticent to speak of himself at all, but over a period of time, piece by piece, we learned much of his story. He was 15 years old in 1938, when his father was put in prison—for whatever reason attendant upon the real reason, which was that he was a Jew. He died in prison ten years later. As an adolescent, then, Avraham resolved in his heart that somehow, someday, he would strike back at the system that had robbed him of his father, and his father of his life. As a young man he was conscripted to a penal battalion. A penal battalion is one made up of children of the "Enemies of the State." The only way out of a penal battalion was by being wounded or by being decorated for bravery. In reality, a penal battalion was a cannon fodder unit whose soldiers had no weapons, much like those of the fanaticized Iranian children during the Iran-Iraq War. When Avraham asked where his weapon was, he was told, "In the hands of the enemy" (of the 800 men in hi battalion, only 100 had weapons. The rest were supposed to capture them from the Germans). When Avraham was later wounded in the right elbow, he was merely transferred to another penal battalion. Avraham was learning that the word of Communist authorities was smoke.

Avraham was again wounded, this time in both legs, and while in the field hospital he made his first break. In those days documentation was a crude and inexact science, and in the hospital Avraham changed his name to "Ibrahim" and the date of his birth from 1923 to 1920. And just like that, Avraham Shifrin disappeared. Ibrahim Shifrin was born, and, having finally made it into the regular army, he eventually became a major. In the regular army he continued studying law (he had studied law one year previously) and was eventually assigned to the Procurator's Office as Chief Investigative Officer involved in civil criminal prosecution for the region of Krasnodar, north of the Black Sea. In his position as prosecutor, Ibrahim sent many people to prison. In the process, he learned the first principle of Soviet justice—it was the poor, petty criminals who were convicted and sent to prison, while Communist Party officials went scot free. Ibrahim's hatred for the Communist system waxed hot and seethed.

Then an opportunity for revenge was finally granted him. A Soviet general whom Ibrahim had gotten off in a certain legal matter, Boris Pastukhov, was promoted to Deputy Minister of the Armaments Ministry, and Ibrahim was soon appointed his legal advisor. And it was in the Armaments Ministry that Ibrahim was given security clearance to view all documents in the super secret "K safe." The K safe documents were the orders signed by Joseph Stalin himself. Ibrahim, in true Oscar Schindler style, befriended the heads of the armament procurement sections for the Navy, Army, Air Force, and rocketry divisions. He learned to give and get favors, and observed how section heads stole super-sensitive technical knowledge from both military and civilian sources, as well as money from their own agencies.

With this information, as well as the secret K file information, Shifrin devised a plan to transmit this information to the West. The only permissible place and occasion to meet foreign diplomats was the Concert. Ibrahim began attending concerts and slipping scraps of paper, on which he had scribbled secret information, into the pockets of passing diplomats. Then, as they say in the trade, a fish came up to bite—an American. And so Ibrahim began working, so to speak, for the Americans. How he once escaped from the clutches of the KGB with the help of then-Ambassador to Russia Charles Bohlen and Vice Counsel McSweeny; how he was captured and imprisoned in Lubyanka Central KGB prison in Moscow, then Lefortovo prison where in 1953, he was sentenced to be shot[30], and then, ten years in the harshest prisons of Siberia, and then into exile in Kazakhstan; how he was released after 17 years with permission to emigrate (and with the expectation that he would soon die); how he survived in Israel and became investigator and researcher into the goings on in the over 2,500 prisons, psychprisons, and slave labor camps of the Soviet Union;[31] and how through the auspices of David Martin of the State Department and Senator Thomas Dodd, he was requested in 1973 to testify concerning those Soviet camps and prisons before the

---

[30] Shifrin was not shot because KGB head Beria and his close subordinants, Gen. Kabulov and Col. Medvedev, Shifrin's chief accusers, were all executed.

[31] Shifrin published The First Guidebook to Prisons and Concentration Camps of the Soviet Union, Bantam Books, New York, 1982.

Sub-Committee on Internal Security of the Judiciary Department of the United States government—all this would require a book in itself.[32]

Safe in Israel, and having married in Israel, Shifrin and his wife Eleanora organized a small group of committed ex-prisoners like himself, working without pay, who by means of friendship, money, and vodka began to infiltrate the secret heart of the Soviet prison system: the KGB computers, and the towns grown up around the larger prisons and camps in Siberia, towns populated by former prisoners and their families who were forbidden to leave Siberia, forever banished from their former homes, towns populated by hungry, vulnerable, vodka-addicted and consequently loose-lipped prison guards. Part of the Shifrins' work was to debrief new immigrants from the Soviet Union who had immigrated to Israel through the auspices of Israel's semi-governmental Jewish Agency.

From a core of committed ex-prisoners, all Jewish, and with the assistance of willing couriers (such as the late "singing" rabbi, Shlomo Carlebach, who often visited the Soviet Union on concert[33])—and even with the help (though not so willing or free) of a certain notorious Russian Mafia personage—the Shifrins in 1989 began receiving, at first in a trickle, and then in a stream, startling news regarding KAL 007 and its passengers.

"Your father may well be alive this day," he told us, speaking clearly, soberly, with no apparent emotion whatsoever. "They may all be alive. Most of them at least were rescued from the plane. Now, those that live, live in gulags."

He indicated that there were signed testimonies, original protocols and interviews. But I was then in no position to judge the worth of his documents. I was trying to judge the integrity of his face. He was cutting open my wife's heart; he was wrecking my life. He was forcing us to remember again what we were only just learning to forget, and he was telling us that it was worse than we had feared.

---

[32] Avraham Shifrin's story is contained in the book, <u>Fourth Dimension</u>, Shamgar Press, Tel Aviv, 1976 (in Hebrew). An English translation will be published shortly.

[33] Personal communication to author from Avraham Shifrin.

He was asking Exie to imagine her father in a prison. I looked him in the eye, and saw nothing but cold sincerity. Exie too was convinced of his honesty. But even crazy people can be sincere. Realizing that he was dependant upon the testimony of others, we requested an interview with one of his sources. He directed us to a young Russian whom Eleanora had debriefed upon his entry to Israel.

Avraham and Eleanora Shifrin—
Investigators of the KAL 007 Shootdown

*   *   *

The morning of August 9, 1991, Exie and I entered the crowded lobby of the Jerusalem Hilton. We had come to meet Reuben V., a former map maker assigned to Soviet Air Defense battery-Military unit 1845. This was the radar unit that, according to Shifrin, had tracked KAL 007 to a safe water landing.

Across the lobby, I noticed a thin blond-haired man rise from his chair and begin making his way toward us. This, I thought, must be Reuben. He seemed to have identified us, most probably knowing that Exie was a Filipino. We approached each other cautiously.

As we exchanged the usual amenities with Reuben, I was struck by this young (he did not look much more than 24), blond, blue-eyed new immigrant's "un-Jewishness." He looked, in fact, Aryan. Later we learned that Reuben's father was Gentile but that his mother was of Jewish birth, making Reuben rabbinically Jewish and thus eligible for citizenship in Israel under the State's Law of Return for all Jews. I—and Exie with me—had recently received citizenship under this law. But I was not yet accustomed to the astounding sight of so many blond blue-eyed immigrants from the former Soviet Union. Immigrants like Reuben would increase Israel's Jewish population in just a few short years from four and a half million to over five million souls.

Then, however, Reuben's unJewishness proved unsettling. Who was he and how much could he be relied on? Could we trust him? Such illiberal sentiments did not disturb me at the time. At the time, they seemed necessary—every bit as necessary as the gun bearer who always accompanied our son Jonathan on his class trips. Life in a border settlement in Israel tends to test one's liberality, and often enough to discard it.

Over many cups of coffee, Reuben struggled with us in Hebrew, English and hand gestures, demonstrating and illustrating on hotel stationary over and over again, attempting to show us the angle of KAL 007's descent at different altitudes as it gradually came down (and here, Reuben's hand was almost flat palm down a few inches from the top of our coffee table) to an altitude Reuben called "Point Zero." We were later to learn that "Point Zero" is about 1,000 feet above the surface of the sea and is the point under which Soviet radar was ineffective due to the curvature of the earth.

Reuben, in such ways, conveyed to us the following story: On September 1, 1983, his commanding officer, while yet a lieutenant on night duty serving at Military Unit 1845 located on Soviet Gavan (the east coast of Russia across from Sakhalin Island), had photographed his radar screen which had been following the flight of KAL 007 for several minutes prior to its being shot down. After missile impact, the radar had continued tracking the jumbo jet for over 12 minutes—until it had descended to Point Zero. The name of Reuben's superior officer was Ryzhkov. Ryzhkov and the whole of Military Unit 1845 were part of the underground staff headquarters located at Komsomolsk-na-amure.

Ryzhkov told Reuben he was certain that KAL 007 had landed safely. Nor was his the only radar station that had followed the flight of the stricken passenger plane to point zero. Another of these was the radar station at Edinke, designated as Air Defense unit 2212 PT6. Reuben drew a map of Soviet Gavan on hotel stationary and placed Edinke northeast of unit 1845. Ryzhkov told Reuben that he had used three rolls of film, each containing 36 exposures, in photographing his radar screen. These rolls, the lieutenant said, were later confiscated by the KGB. All personnel at Unit 1845 as well as at the other radar stations were commanded to maintain silence concerning the tracking of KAL 007. Everyone understood that the penalty for disobeying this order would be death or exile.

"Why would anyone tell you all this?" I asked him. "Especially in light of the penalties?"

"He was drunk," Reuben told us. "And he was bitter. They had humiliated him—he had been passed over for promotion while others involved in the incident went up a grade. And when he inquired of the KGB why this was so, they told him that it was because he had failed to load the camera. But Ryzhkov knew better."

All this was told to Reuben when he served under Ryzhkov—sometime during 1987—1989. Subsequently, Ryzhkov had finally received a promotion, being made captain and commander of the same Unit 1845. Reuben thought that Captain Ryzhkov was later assigned to Mariinskoe, just north of Komsomolsk-na-amure.

Ryzhkov. Valery Vladimirovich Ryzhkov. This name was to reappear in a top secret CIA document undertaken as a Republican Staff Study. The existence of this document was first disclosed in the South Korean Parliament in October of 1992 by Korean legislator and opposition leader Sonn Se-Il, and Reuters News Service published portions of it on October 26, 1992.[34] The document mentions reports by new Russian immigrants to Israel concerning "several Soviet Air Defense Radar Sites on the Soviet mainland opposite Sakhalin" which "simultaneously tracked the gradual descent of KAL 007." The report continues, "For example, then Lieutenant Valery Vladimirovich Ryzhkov was the duty officer the night KAL 007 went down at Radio Technical Brigade 1845 at the Town of Zavet Ilyicha on the mainland coast. He personally tracked KAL 007 in its controlled descent to the water, and he was in communication with at least three other Air Defense radar sites and several Soviet KGB border guard boats which also tracked KAL 007 in its controlled descent."[35]

Within just a few weeks of our interview with Reuben, the question propelling us had subtly but substantially changed. No longer was it, "Where are the bodies?" The question had now become, "Where are the survivors? Where is Tay?"

---

[34] Since disclosure of this document and publication of portions of the summary in October of 1992, various parts of the whole report have been quoted by the media. The CIA neither confirms nor denies the authenticity of the report. Its authenticity is discussed and affirmed in Chapter 6.

[35] "Top Secret/Codeword CIA Report," p. 76.

CHAPTER 2

Impact Plus 104 Seconds

"The target is destroyed," Major Osipovich said. "I am breaking off attack."

But Osipovich, winging his way back to Sokol Airbase on Sakhalin, was mistaken.

In a two-second interval, the Soviet pilot launched two R-98 (ANAB) air-to-air missiles. The first missile was designed to "home in" onto the exhaust of aircraft engines, exploding on contact. As the evidence will show, this missile completely missed. The second missile was radar-controlled and designed to detonate 50 meters from an aircraft. It exploded at exactly 6:26:02—exactly five hours, 26 minutes and 18 seconds after KAL 007 began its taxi to takeoff from Anchorage, Alaska. (Osipovich delayed a number of seconds in his reporting). We are able to reconstruct events with great detail from this point on.

Almost immediately upon detonation, KAL 007's nose pitched gradually up until, 23 seconds after missile detonation, it was at its greatest angle—15 degrees. At the same time, the plane gradually arced upward until, 48 seconds after detonation, it was at an altitude of 38,250 feet. From that point, the aircraft began its downward leg of the arc for approximately 25 seconds, until it reached the altitude it maintained prior to missile impact—approximately 35,000 feet. The entire arc lasted one minute and 13 seconds.

The arc was moderate enough that any passenger standing would probably not have been thrown to the floor, though food and drink would have toppled over and slipped off the trays. The reason for this arc was damage to the tail of the aircraft. The crossover cable from the left inboard elevator to the right outboard elevator was damaged causing the cable to unravel.

From the Cockpit Voice tapes, we can see the struggle into which Captain Chun and his copilot were immediately thrown:

Captain: (6:26:06)
What happened?

Copilot: (6:26:08)
What?

Captain: (6:26:10)
Retard throttles.

Copilot: (6:26:11)
Engines normal, sir.[36]

From this last statement by the copilot, it is evident that the heat-seeking missile, which would have homed in on one of the engines, missed. This is verified by the Digital Flight Data Recorder. At 11 seconds after missile impact, the Cabin Altitude Warning Alert sounds. Air has been rushing out of the punctured fuselage. The fact that it took as much as eleven seconds after impact before the alert sounded indicates that the total area of damage to the passenger compartment of the aircraft was only 1 3/4 square feet.[37]

As the missile hadn't hit the fuselage itself, but rather exploded 50 meters away, that 1.75 square feet area was probably made up of many small puncture holes caused by flying fragments—all toward the rear of the fuselage. Congressman Larry McDonald, seated in an

---

[36] KAL 007 CVR Transcript, p. 13.

[37] ICAO Report 1993, p. 54. "Eleven seconds after the CAM recorded the first sounds of the attack, the sound of the cabin altitude warning was heard... It was possible to estimate the approximate area of holes which would result in a decompression and subsequent cabin altitude warning after eleven seconds. An estimate, taking into account the output of the air-conditioning packs, indicated holes with a total area in the order of 1.75 square feet."

aisle seat of the first class section—as well as Exie's father and cousin, seated in row 40 over the wings—were most likely unharmed. Furthermore, it would have been impossible for anyone to have been sucked out of the plane, though there may well have been wounded or dead in the rear section struck by missile fragments[38].

What were the passengers and crew experiencing at this time? There have been many conjectures, ranging from "nothing, as they had all died in the explosion," to "undergoing the excruciating pains of asphyxiation at high altitude." These conjectures are incorrect. Certainly, fear would have run through the passengers, and there would have been many prayers for safety and salvation. But there was a sufficient supply of oxygen for comfortable breathing. Aviation Specialist Dr. Malcolm Brenner[39] explains:

"Crew members and passengers would have about one minute of expected useful consciousness unless they successfully began receiving oxygen from an oxygen mask."[40]

Well within that critical "one minute of expected useful consciousness," the oxygen masks had already dropped and, because of the upward pitch of the aircraft's nose for most of its ascent leg of the arc, the masks were drifting back toward or behind the heads of the passengers, within easy reach. If airline regulations, routinely demonstrated by the flight attendants, were followed by the passengers, adults would have donned their masks first before putting them on their children.

At 6:26:34, thirty-two seconds after missile detonation, the following consecutive messages were broadcast over the public address system in English, Korean, and Japanese: "Attention, Emergency Descent. Put out your cigarette. This is an Emergency Descent. Put

---

[38] It would have been impossible for anyone to be sucked out of a hole (assuming one hole instead of many small punctures) of only 1 ¾ foot area. Compare with TWA Flight 840 (Boeing 727) with a 4 foot hole in its side blown open by a bomb. Three adults and a child were sucked out and found on the ground 15,000 feet below.

[39] Associated with Aviation Safety Association International, a firm in the aviation accident investigation field.

[40] KAL 007—The Coverup by David Pearson (Summit Books: New York, 1987) p. 77.

the mask on your nose and mouth and adjust the headbands." When Captain Chun radioed Tokyo Airport, one minute and two seconds after missile detonation, his voice was already muffled as he was then speaking through the mike located in his oxygen mask[41], "Korean Air 007 ah . . . We are . . . Rapid compressions. Descend to 10,000."

Furthermore, if the passengers and crew had not been fitted out with oxygen masks and sufficient oxygen supply, Captain Chun would have sought to descend to 5,000 meters (16,400 feet), not 10,000, because it is generally recognized by all airlines that it is only from 5,000 meters that it is possible to breath unassisted by oxygen masks.

The rest of the one minute and 13 second arc—and the subsequent leveling out at pre-missile impact altitude—display the remarkable ability of the pilots to control the damaged aircraft. With only one of the four hydraulic systems fully operational (making control difficult, but by no means impossible)[42], and with wing flaps up, "control was reduced to the right inboard aileron and the innermost of the spoiler section on each side."[43] From 17 to 40 seconds after missile impact, the pilots struggled unsuccessfully to bring the plane to a lower altitude.

Captain: (6:26:24)
Altitude is going up, altitude is going up![44]

Captain: (6:26:25)
Speed brake is coming out.

Copilot: (6:26:26)
What? What?

---

[41] "Accentuated breathing during the transmission indicated that an oxygen mask was being worn." ICAO Report, 1993, p. 35.

[42] See Appendix E, p. 161, for the detailed substantiation for the above assertion.

[43] ICAO Report, 1993, p. 54.

[44] See Appendix E, p. 161 for a reconstruction of the drama taking place in the cockpit—using simultaneous Cockpit Voice Recorder and Digital Flight Recorder tapes.

Captain: (6:26:29)
Check it out.

(6:26:30)
[*Sound of Public address and chime for automatic cabin announcement.*]

Copilot: (6:26:33)
[*Sound of cabin call*] I am not able to drop altitude—now unable.

Captain: (6:26:38)
Altitude is going up.

Captain: (6:26:40)
This is not working. This is not working!

(Captain Chun now switches off the autopilot in order to manually move the column forward to bring down the airplane.)

Captain: (6:26:41)
Manually.

Copilot: (6:26:42)
Cannot do manually.

(Captain Chun has now moved the column forward but the plane has not responded. It is still ascending.)

Copilot: (6:26:43)
Not working manually, also.

Copilot: (6:26:45)
Engines are normal, sir.

(This is the second announcement of the normal operational functioning of the engines.)[45]

It is at this point in their struggle that Captain Chun succeeds in bringing the plane on its downward leg of the arc. It is not evident from the Digital Flight Data Recorder exactly how Captain Chun has succeeded but, nose down, KAL 007 begins to rapidly accelerate. It continues to pick up speed until, at a point almost exactly at KAL 007's pre-hit altitude, Captain Chun quickly reduces the plane's downward acceleration, sharply raising the pitch of the nose for eight seconds. He then levels the plane out. After maintaining this altitude for 16 seconds, he points the nose of the plane gently down for a graduated descent.[46] This, then, is the end of the minute and 44 second tape handed to the International Civil Aviation Organization by Boris Yeltsin and the Russian Federation.

Good work, Captain Chun!

This beginning of perhaps the most remarkably documented air emergency and descent—a descent which was to last for at least 12 minutes—indicates that KAL 007 had a good measure of both potential and actual controllability. Seven indications of this controllability are:

1. Sufficient oxygen for pilot alertness.

2. All engines were operating normally.

3. Electrical system was operative (otherwise the radio and engines would not have operated).

4. Demonstrated pilot ability to decrease speed of KAL 007 in its downward phase (If he would not have been able to do so, the aircraft would continue to increase its downward acceleration—only to collide with the water in from

---

[45] ICAO Report, 1993, KAL 007 CVR Transcript, p. 13.
[46] See annotated Digital Flight Data Recorder Chart in Appendix G.

2 to 2 1/2 minutes. (KAL 007's flight lasted at least 12 minutes).[47]

5. KAL 007 was able to regain its pre-hit altitude almost exactly. (It is highly unlikely that KAL 007 regained exact altitude after its arc by chance.)

6. KAL 007 was able to regain its pre-missile hit rate of forward acceleration.

7. Captain Chun was able to bring KAL 007's nose (pitch) to the plane's exact level of flight.

These many key parameters of aircraft controllability were met at the beginning of KAL 007's post-impact flight. More would be met during the calculated and graduated duration of the over-twelve-minutes flight[48]—until the aircraft rested safely on the water's surface off Moneron Island.

Questions remain, however. Why did the Russians hand over only one minute and forty-four seconds of the post impact phase of the flight? Unlike ordinary recording tapes, Black Box tapes do not "run out." Recording on loops that recycle every 30 minutes, they do not come to an end. Furthermore, a midair explosion or crash did not

---

[47] On October 31st, 1999, Egypt Air Flight 990, a Boeing 767 with a complement of 217 passengers and crew on a flight from New York to Cairo, crashed off Nantucket Island in the Atlantic Ocean. Radar trackings show that the plane took just 36 seconds to fall 13,900 feet—from 33,000 feet to 19,100 feet (a fall of about 386 feet per second or about 23,160 feet per minute. With a truly plunging and increasingly accelerating Egypt Air flight 990 as our comparison and control, if KAL 007 had in fact been plunging out of control and its flight had lasted at least twelve minutes (verified by radar trackings) its altitude would have had to be an absurd 277,920 feet, not 35,000 feet, its altitude when rocketed. Compare, also, the fall of a Chinese Airline 747 on Feb. 20, 1985, of 32,000 feet, from 41,000 feet to 9,000 feet (falling about 267 feet per second. This fall took only slightly less than 2 minutes.

[48] See full list on page 74.

terminate the recording, since radar followed KAL 007 in its flight for many minutes after these tapes ended. Where are the tapes for the remainder of 007's fateful flight? What could the Russians be trying to hide? But for now the question remains, "Why did the tape end just then?" Or, in the politically neutralized words of the United Nations' International Civil Aviation Organization, "It could not be established why both flight recorders simultaneously ceased to operate 104 seconds after the attack. The power supply cables were fed to the rear of the aircraft in raceways on *opposite* [*present author's emphasis*] sides of the fuselage until they came together behind the two recorders."[49]

It is highly unlikely that separate electric cables at opposite sides of a fuselage would be struck by missile fragments at the same second.

The Japanese radar facility located on the northernmost Japanese Island of Wakkanai had also tracked KAL 007 in its descent. The Wakkanai facility trackings were published by the International Civil Aviation Organization in December, 1983. These trackings, combined with Soviet trackings (perhaps including the tracking recorded by Lieutenant Ryzhkov's unit 1845 at Komsomolsk-na-amure), were the basis of both Secretary of State George Shultz's and acting Permanent Representative of the U.S.A. to the U.N. Charles Liechtenstein's assertions that the Soviets did indeed shoot down KAL 007 and that the plane disappeared from radar scopes at precisely 6:38 a.m. (12 minutes after missile impact). In identical words they asserted on September 1, 1983, "At 18:26, the Soviet pilot reported that he fired a missile and the target was destroyed. At 18:30 hours, the Korean aircraft was reported by radar an altitude of 5,000 meters. At 18:38 hours, the Korean plane disappeared from the radar screens."[50]

But the trackings prove something far more important than these

[49] I.C.A.O. Report 1993, p. 55.

[50] From Soviet ground-to-ground communications during the time of the shootdown appended to the International Civil Aviation Organization (ICAO) 1993 report, it is clear that KAL 007 was last located at 5,000 meters altitude at 6:33 a.m.—not at 6:30 a.m.—and it was still being tracked by Soviet radar over Moneron Island at 6:34 a.m. Information paper no. 1, p. 135.

assertions. They prove conclusively that KAL 007's emergency descent was a well-controlled descent conforming to standard procedures designed to ensure the safety of passengers and crew. From these trackings, we can presume the safe water landing of KAL 007 and the safety of its passengers.

These published trackings indicate that the descent was made in three stages:

1.   There was a rapid five minute descent, from 35,000 feet to 16,400 feet. The plane was dropping at an average rate of 3,700 feet per minute or 42 miles an hour. This first stage ended exactly at the altitude at which it would be possible to breathe without the support of oxygen masks. Having reached that altitude, the second stage began.

2.   KAL 007 slowed its descent and for four minutes—from 16,400 ft. to 5,000 ft—the plane dropped at an average rate of 2,875 ft. per minute or 32.6 miles per hour.

3.   The third stage lasted for at least[51] a period of three minutes. KAL 007 flew from 5,000 ft. to 1,000 ft. dropping at an average rate of 1,333 ft per minute or 26 miles an hour. This rate of descent is standard operating procedure designed to allow the search for a suitable landing area. In the case of KAL 007, "suitable landing" also included positioning the plane parallel to the waves and, if at all possible, alighting, with tail slightly pointed down, on the waves' crests, rather than in the hollow, in order to avoid being swamped.

The CIA report concludes that "there was clearly a decelerating average rate of descent, rather than an accelerating rate of descent. This declining rate of descent shows that KAL 007 was not in a

---

[51] "At least," because there is no way of knowing how much longer KAL 007 flew while below point 0.

plummet or crash dive and is another indication that KAL 007 was under some degree of control by the pilot."[52]

*   *   *

Yet there is one related datum that would seem to controvert KAL 007's safe landing. Early in the morning of September 1, the *Chidori Maru*, No. 58, a 99 ton Japanese Cuttlefish boat under command of Captain Shizuka Hayashi, was plying its way in an east northeast heading coordinates 46°34'N, 141°16'E, twenty-two and a half miles north of Moneron Island, a small island in the Tatar Straits west of Sakhalin island. At approximately 6:30 local time, fishermen heard an explosion and then saw a light that flashed for five seconds low on the horizon. They described it as a glowing orange colored, expanding fireball. They also described hearing either one or two explosions coming after the fireball. These explosions were fainter than the first and were accompanied by faint flashes. It is not clear if the International Civil Aviation Organization's report of 1993 that "the aircraft was destroyed on impact with the sea, the impact was not survivable," was substantially influenced by the testimony of the *Chidori Maru* crew. In fact, the *Chidori Maru* testimony says nothing about "impact with the sea," but rather an explosion in the air.[53]

Whatever may be said of the explosion seen near the water and heard by the crew of the *Chidori Maru*—an explosion 22 1/2 miles away from Moneron island at 6:30 in the morning—one thing is certain: it could not have been that of KAL 007. For at 6:30 a.m., KAL 007 was high in the skies frantically being searched for by Soviet interceptors. At 6:34 a.m., four minutes after the Chidori Maru crew had witnessed the destruction of something, KAL was located at an altitude of 5,000 meters (16,400 feet) and turning. It was exactly at this altitude that KAL 007 had sharply decelerated retarding its rush downward as it had already reached "breathing" altitude.

---

[52] "Top Secret/Codeword CIA Report," p. 46.

[53] This is the only eyewitness evidence for the destruction of KAL 007 provided by ICAO's 1983 and 1993 reports.

The survival of KAL 007 past 6:30 a.m. is amply and dramatically proven by telecommunication transcripts recording the interchange between General Kornukov of the Far East Military District directing the destruction of KAL 007 and Lieutenant Colonel Gerasimenko, Acting Commander of 41st Fighter Regiment. These transcripts were annexed to the International Civil Aviation Organization's report of 1993 but barely commented upon. (The combined Russian and Japanese radar trackings showing that KAL 007 was being tracked until 6:38 a.m. also rule out the relevancy of the *Chidori Maru* sighting.)[54]

General Kornukov: (6:33)
Hurry up, guys, that's a real target. Hello Mastak [*Radio call sign*], Mastak, Mastak, Mastak, Mastak, Mastak, Mastak, Mastak, Mastak.

Gerasimenko:
Gerasimenko, altitude of target is 5,000.

Kornukov:
5,000 already?

Gerasimenko: (6:34)
Affirmative, turning left, right, apparently . . . it is descending.

Kornukov:
Destroy it, use the 23 [*MiG*], destroy it, I said!

Gerasimenko:
Roger, destroy it.

Kornukov:
Well, where is the fighter? How far from the target?

---

[54] See Chapter 5, pg. 95, for the discussion of the "mini-war" explanation for the *Chidori Maru* sighting.

Gerasimenko:
Comrade General, they cannot see the target.
Kornukov:
They cannot see the target?[55]

And so KAL 007 continued its flight for many minutes beyond the *Chidori Maru* sighting, eluding Soviet interceptors but not coastal radar trackings, until it gradually dropped below point zero, just 1,000 feet above the surface of waters off the small island of Moneron.

What then, did the crew of the Japanese cuttlefish boat see in the east northeast horizon? Could there have been other planes in the area, and could these have been Soviet and U.S. warplanes engaged in aerial combat in which KAL 007—innocently or not—had been caught, as some commentators have suggested?[56] Was the explosion witnessed by the *Chidori Maru* one of those participants in a drama in which the cold war had suddenly turned hot? And could this explain the sobriety in Senator Jesse Helm's letter of December 10, 1991 to Boris Yeltsin, in which he stated, "The KAL 007 tragedy was one of the most tense incidents of the entire cold war"?[57]

The next stage of KAL 007's descent and General Kornukov's frantic and futile attempt to destroy it seem taken more from an imaginative thriller then from authenticated documents. Yet, it happened in real life and these documents are available for our examination.

---

[55] ICAO Report, 1993, p. 136.

[56] Michel Brun in his book Incident at Sakhalin: The True Mission of KAL Flight 007, (Four Walls Eight Windows, New York, 1995).

[57] The complete text of Senator Helm's letter to Boris Yeltsin is in Appendix F.

CHAPTER 3

Lost Over Moneron

Major Osipovich, returning to Sokol Air Base on Sakhalin, believed his mission accomplished. But quite a different conclusion was being drawn by several Soviet radar command posts. For within seconds—and for minutes after—after Osipovich had given his report, KAL 007 could clearly be seen still flying rather than disappearing from the screen, as would have been the case if there had been a midair explosion. Furthermore, according to the Digital Flight Data Recorder tape, the jumbo jet was actually climbing.[58]

General Kornukov: (6:26)
Do you see the target on the screen?

Lt. Col. Gerasimenko:
We can see [*it*] for the moment.

Kornukov:
Did he fire both missiles or one?

Gerasimenko:
Both missiles . . .

Kornukov:
Bring in the MiG 23.

Kornukov:
Gerasimenko!

[58] See Digital Flight Data Recorder chart in Appendix G.

Gerasimenko:
Yes.

Kornukov: (6:27)
This is the task . . . Bring the MiG 23 in to destroy the target.

Gerasimenko:
Yes, Sir.

Kornukov:
Gerasimenko.

Gerasimenko:
163 [*designation for MiG 23*] has been ordered to engage afterburner.
We are bringing him to attack position.

Kornukov:
Roger. Did Osipovich see the missiles explode? Hello?

Gerasimenko:
He fired two missiles.

Kornukov:
Ask him, ask him yourself, get on channel 3 and ask Osipovich, did
he or did he not see the explosions?

Gerasimenko:
Right away.[59]

According to United States electronic intelligence intercepts,
Osipovich was asked at 6:27, "805, did you launch one missile or
both?" Osipovich replied, "I launched both." But within two minutes

[59] Report of the Completion of the Fact Finding Investigation Regarding the Shoot
down of Korean Airline Boeing 747 (Flight KE007) on 31 Aug. 1983. Information paper no. 1. United Nation Security Council-139th session, 1993, pp.
131, 132.

of impact, concern about the airliner's survival had spread to other command posts. Still at 6:26, when, according to the Soviet and Japanese radar sightings and the Digital Flight Data Recorder, KAL 007 was about to begin its five minute accelerated descent to attain normal breathing altitude, Lt. Col. Novoseletski, the Commander of Smirnykh Air Base, expresses that concern to Titovnin, Maj. Osipovich's ground controller.

Lt. Col. Novoseletski: (6:26)
Titovnin, well, what is happening?

Titovnin:
Nothing for the moment.

Novoseletski:
Well, what is happening, what is the matter, who guided him in, he locked on, why didn't he shoot it down?

Titovnin:
They fired. They fired. We are now waiting for the result, Comrade Colonel.[60]

At 6:28, General Kornukov has been made aware not only of KAL 007's survival, but also of its maneuverability.

Gerasimenko:
The target turned to the north.

Kornukov:
The target turned to the north?

Gerasimenko:
Affirmative.

---

[60] ibid., p. 88.

Kornukov:
Bring the 23 [*MiG*] in to destroy it!

By 6:29, General Kornukov is furious over the failure to down KAL 007, and he lashes out at Lt. Col. Gerasimenko. His speech and his thoughts have become confused.

Gerasimenko:
Comrade right turn.

Kornukov:
Well, I understand, I do not understand the result, why is the target flying? Missiles were fired. Why is the target flying? [*obscenities*] Well, what is happening?

Gerasimenko:
Yes.

Kornukov:
Well, I am asking, give the order to the Controller, what is wrong with you there? Have you lost your tongues?

Gerasimenko:
Comrade General, I gave the order to the Chief of Staff, the Chief of Staff to the Controller, and the Controller is giving the order to . . .

Kornukov: (6:30)
Well, how long does it take for this information to get through, well, what, [*you*] cannot ask the results of firing the missiles, where, what, did [*he*] not understand or what?[61]

The transcripts indicate that from 6:30 to 6:34 there is mounting concern at the failure to down KAL 007. But, beginning at 6:34, another concern begins to dominate at the various command posts—

---

[61] ibid., p. 133.

KAL 007 has disappeared from the radar scopes! Neither do the interceptors have visual or radar contact with the jumbo jet. That this was not caused by any midair mishap in the flight of KAL 007 is clear from Soviet radar trackings other than those reported in the annexed telecommunications—trackings that record KAL 007's flight as lasting at least until 6:38. It is these other trackings which were the basis of United States State Department and United Nations assertions that KAL 007 was in the air for at least 12 minutes after it had been rocketed.

At 6:34, then, eight minutes after missile impact, "attack" radar has lost contact with Flight 007, never again to regain it. KAL 007 is at this time at 16,400 feet altitude (5,000 meters).

Kornukov:
Destroy it, use the 23 to destroy it, I said!

Gerasimenko:
Roger, destroy it.

Kornukov:
Well, where is the fighter, how far from the target?

Gerasimenko:
Comrade General, they cannot see the target.

Kornukov:
They cannot see the target?[62]

For a full two minutes, radar station after radar station, responding to queries, verify that they are no longer tracking KAL 007. Then, at 6:36, ten minutes after missile impact, we are informed by General Kornukov exactly where KAL 007 is located. It is located over the island of Moneron.

---

[62] ibid., p. 135.

Kornukov: (6:36)
O [*obscenities*] well you know the range where the Target is, it is over
   Moneron.[63]

KAL 007 had passed from Soviet territory over Sakhalin Island,
where it had been rocketed, and had entered into international waters
only to once again enter Soviet territory as it approached Moneron
Island. There is no doubt that Soviet commanders knew exactly where
Flight 007 was and, in effect, any "search" operation they would conduct could only be a rescue operation.

Titovnin: (6:38)
They lost the target, Comrade Colonel, in the area of Moneron.

Novoseletski:
In the area of Moneron?

Titovnin:
The pilots do not see it, neither the one nor the other. The radio
   forces have reported. RTF has reported that after the launch, the
   target entered a right turn over Moneron.

Novoseletski:
Uh-huh.

Titovnin:
Descending.
And lost over Moneron . . .

Novoseletski:
So, the task. They say it has violated the State border again now?

Titovnin:
Well, it is the area of Moneron, of course, over our territory.

---

[63] ibid., p. 136.

Novoseletski:
Get it! Get it! Go ahead bring in the MiG 23.

Titovnin:
Roger. The MiG 23 is in that area. It is descending to 5,000 [*meters*].
The order has been given. Destroy upon detection.[64]

Moneron. To have been located over Moneron is to have been pinpointed. Moneron is a small, rocky island in the Tatar Straits, approximately 4 miles long (north-south axis) and 3 miles wide. It is located about 30 miles west-southwest of Sakhalin's port city of Nevelsk, and about 26 miles due west of Sakhalin's nearest coastal point.

We all have our ways of visualizing, of helping our imagination. In Israel, I have often spent an evening on the boardwalk of the town of Tiberias located on the western shore of the Sea of Galilee. Directly across from Tiberias on the eastern shore of the Sea of Galilee, I can see the lights of the fishing village and vacation resort of Ein Gev. The width of the Sea of Galilee at this point is somewhat over eight miles. It is easy for me to locate its midpoint. From where I stand in Tiberias, then, to that midpoint is the whole length of Moneron Island. Moneron is small, indeed!

According to eyewitness testimony contained in the 1991 *Izvestiya* series on KAL 007, as well as eyewitness accounts reported by Japanese fishermen, KAL 007 made two turns around Moneron Island.[65] These turns might have been made while the aircraft was still descending—that is, KAL 007 was spiraling—or they might have been made while the aircraft was at constant altitude—that is, circling. In either case, the circumference of KAL 007's flight path could not have been much greater than the four-mile length of the island itself, because the aircraft's circling could only have been in anticipation of and preparatory to landing close enough to Moneron to ensure rescue. This is especially forceful as we remember that KAL 007 was last located by the Soviets as being "over Moneron" and "descending."

[64] ibid., p. 90.
[65] Top Secret/Codeword CIA Republican Staff Study, p. 49.

Three things are clear from these observations:

1. The "search" missions sent out by the Soviets could only
   have been rescue missions,

2. The United States and Japanese Search and Rescue operations in international waters at least a full twelve and a
   half miles north of Moneron at its nearest point and
   encompassing a full 22.5 square mile area could only be
   futile (as, indeed, it proved to be).

3. The main Russian salvage operations, at coordinates 46°
   33' 32" N—141°19' 41" E, in international waters, a full
   17 nautical miles north of Moneron Island, could only
   have been diversionary.

But to KAL 007's true position, Moneron Island itself, there were, indeed, at least two Soviet rescue operations sent out within minutes of KAL 007's downing. These missions are documented in the Russian ground-to-ground telecommunications transcripts, and in view of the specificity of KAL 007's location, there is no reason to doubt their success. The first mission involved rescue helicopters, border guards and the KGB, and was ordered at 6:47 a.m., just 21 minutes after missile impact and nine minutes after KAL 007 had reached point zero altitude.

Novoseletski: (6:47)
You don't have the sunrise there yet?

Titovnin:
No, it will be in about thirty minutes.

Novoseletski:
Prepare whatever helicopters there are. Rescue helicopters.

Titovnin:
Rescue?

Novoseletski:
Yes. And there will probably be a task set for the area where the
target was lost.

Titovnin:
Roger. Is this to be done through your SAR [*Search and Rescue*]?

Novoseletski:
Eh?

Titovnin:
Assign the task to Chaika through your SAR, Comrade Colonel,
Khomutovo[66] does not come under us and neither does
Novoaleksandrovska. We have nothing here.

Novoseletski:
Very well.

Titovnin:
Novoaleksandrovska must be brought to readiness and Khomutovo.
The border guards and KGB are at Khomutovo.[67]

"Chaika" is the call sign of the Far East Military District (FEMD)
Air Force Command Post. Consequently, this first documented rescue
mission could only be effected by order of the FEMD, which was
second in jurisdiction to the Soviet Far East Military Theatre of Operations. Neither the shooting down nor the rescue of Flight 007
was, therefore, of local decision.

---

[66] Civilian and military airport at Yuzhno-Sakhalinsk City in southern Sakhalin.

[67] Report of the Completion of the Fact Finding Investigation Regarding the Shoot
down of Korean Airline Boeing 747 (Flight KE007) on 31 Aug. 1983. Information paper no. 1. United Nation Security Council-139th session, 1993, p.
93.

The second mission involved the civilian ships in the vicinity of Moneron as well as the border guards. This mission was ordered at 6:55; just 29 minutes after missile impact and 17 minutes after KAL 007 had reached point zero altitude.

Gen. Strogov:[68](6:54)

Hello . . . Hello, Titovnin . . . You s . . . [*obscenities*] I'll lock you up in the guard house. Why don't you pick up the phone?

Titovnin:

Comrade General, everyone was busy here.

Strogov:

You have nothing there to be busy with. Busy! What kind of nonsense is that? So, where is Kornukov?

Titovnin:

Kornukov is here.

Strogov:

Put him on the phone.

Titovnin:

One minute. He is reporting to Kamenski,[69] Comrade General.

Strogov: (6:55)

So, what you need to do now. Contact these . . . [*obscenities*], these sailors, these, what do you . . . [*obscenities*]?

Titovnin:

Border guards?

---

[68] Deputy Commander of the Far East Military District.

[69] Commander of Far East Military District Air Force. This is more evidence that the shoot-down of KAL 007 and the rescue of its passengers were not decisions made by local commanders but emanated from the highest echelons of the Soviet military.

Strogov:
Huh?

Titovnin:
Border guards?

Strogov:
Well, the civilian sailors.

Titovnin:
Understood.

Strogov:
The border guards. What ships do we now have near Moneron Island, if they are civilians, send [*them*] there immediately.[70]

Titovnin:
Understood, Comrade General.[71]

This second of the documented, authorized rescue missions was also ordered by highest authority. General Strogov was directly subordinate to General Ivan Moiseevich Tretyak, the Commander of the Far East Military District. (It was with General Tretyak that General Vladimir L. Govrov, the Commander of the Far East Theatre of Operations had come into agreement that the "intruder" aircraft must be shot down.)[72]

---

[70] Note the consistency of Strogov's site identification with Kornukov's. Both generals simply specify it as "Moneron." Ships that are already "near Moneron" are sent to Moneron itself—not to coordinates eleven miles away.

[71] ibid., pp. 95, 96.

[72] Among the ground-to-ground communications appended to the 1993 ICAO Report, the following conversation (unidentified speakers) is recorded at 6:45:
    "Weapons were used, weapons authorized at the highest level.
    Ivan Moiseevich authorized it. Hello, hello."
    "Say again."
    "I cannot hear you clearly now."

Shoes

But what indications are there that the passengers of Korean Air Lines 007 were prepared for an emergency landing on water—a landing which they hoped to survive and from which they hoped to be rescued? Indeed, there are indications not only of preparations but of successful rescue as well. These indications may be summed up in one word—shoes! Shoes in which there were no feet—and, of course, no bodies attached to those nonexistent feet! The pictures in the 1983 end-of-the-year annual edition of *Life Magazine* tell it all. A pile of shoes, sandals, and sneakers, new and old, part of the flotsam of the crash which was displayed at a prefecture office in the city of Sapporo, on the northernmost Japanese island of Hokkaido. This footwear had been worn by the passengers the day they boarded their flight. Sonia and Joe Munder are shown holding two differing sneakers, one for each of Sonia's children, Christian, age 14, and Lisi, age 17. Sonia had no difficulty recognizing the sneakers because of the intricate way her children laced them. In a personal conversation with the author, she affirms that these were the sneakers her children had worn for Flight 007. In similar vein, *Izvestiya* Correspondent Alexandr Shalnev recounts a conversation with a mother (identified only as A.) of a KAL 007 victim.

> "A. said: 'In one of the pictures. I recognized my daughter's sneakers . . .'
>
> I was surprised: 'How could you recognize them?'
>
> 'I recognized them just like that. You see, there are all kinds of inconspicuous marks which strangers do not notice. This is how I recognized them. My daughter loved to wear them.' "[73]

"He gave the order. Hello, hello, hello."

"Yes, yes."

"Ivan Moiseevich gave the order, Tretyak."

"Roger, roger."

"Weapons were used at his order."

[73] Izvestiya, February 1991, p. 7.

What these "peopleless" shoes indicate is that the KAL 007 passengers had been instructed to remove their shoes in anticipation of a water evacuation by sliding down the aircraft's chutes—an evacuation procedure that passengers aboard transoceanic flights are early in their flight acquainted with through standardized motion picture presentations. The instruction to remove footwear would probably have been given sometime after the first five minutes of descent, as radar trackings indicate that prior to that, KAL 007's angle of descent would have been too great.

Soviet Explanations

That these shoes were returned while corpses were not indicates that the rescue operations were successful. Russian commentators have been pained in their attempts to explain the virtual disappearance of KAL 007's 269 passengers and crew from the scene of what they claim is the underwater wreckage. There are four theories that the Soviets have contrived. The earliest was that there were no bodies found because KAL 007 had but a small complement of military personnel and no civilian passengers. This first version of the spy plane theory was by and large discarded by September 9, 1983, when Marshal Nicolay Ogarkov, U.S.S.R. Chief of General Staff and First Deputy Defense Minister, conceded that there had been civilian passengers aboard KAL 007.

In his press conference of September 9, 1983, as quoted by Moscow Radio of the same date, Ogarkov stated, "It has been proved irrefutably that the intrusion of the plane of the South Korean Airlines into Soviet airspace was a deliberately, thoroughly planned intelligence operation. It was directed from certain centers in the territory of the United States and Japan. A civilian plane was chosen for its deliberately, disregarding or, possibly, counting on loss of human life."

The anguish of thousands of relatives and friends of the victims of KAL 007 had also discredited this non-civilian passenger theory from the start.

The second theory maintains that there were no bodies because they were thoroughly pulverized either in a midair explosion or a catastrophic crash at sea. A thorough pulverization of bodies is untenable, never having occurred before or since. The crew of the space shuttle Challenger is more the rule. At an even slightly higher altitude than KAL 007, the Challenger did have a cataclysmic midair explosion and did have a subsequent catastrophic crash into the sea. Yet, all the bodies were not only recovered but also identifiable, however smashed. Subsequent to KAL 007's downing, midair explosions and subsequent crashes at sea of other Boeing 747 jumbo jets did occur.[74] The aftermath of these latter incidents are illuminating for our understanding of what occurred with KAL 007. Many bodies were immediately recovered at the latter crash sites and all were identified! This last point is telling, as a full eight days after the shootdown just two partial bodies and 11 small body parts would be washed up at the Japanese shore—all unidentifiable. These few small body parts in themselves, therefore, serve to support the contention of passenger and crew rescue, a mute but horrific testimony of how far the Soviets might go to cover up passenger rescue. It is not inconceivable that the people represented by these 13 body parts were killed for the purpose of Soviet cover-up. Most devastating to any passenger pulverization theory, from examination of the Black Box tapes handed over by the Russian Federation to the United Nations in 1993, it is clear that KAL 007, in fact, did not explode on missile impact and a crash at sea merely postulated—wrongly.

The third theory for the virtual disappearance of 269 people from the site of the alleged crash is truly ludicrous but is included here as it is suggested by Soviet correspondent Andrey Illesh in his book, *The*

---

[74] The closest parallels are the crashes of the South African Airways Boeing 747 on November 28, 1987, and Air India Boeing 747, blown up by a terrorist bomb over the North Atlantic on June 23, 1985.

Mystery of Korean Boeing 747. This theory proposes that the bodies were eaten by giant crabs. There is even a picture of one of those crabs that supposedly populate the sea bottom where KAL 007 finally came to rest. But what of the bones? How did these crabs dispose of them?! The crab theory has been persistent and has been echoed by the Soviet interceptor pilot Gennadie Osipovich himself (though evidently not with full conviction).

" . . . I heard that they had found the 'Boeing' when I was still on Sakhalin. And even investigated it. But no one saw people there. I, however, explain that by the fact that there are crabs in the sea off Sakhalin that immediately devour everything . . . I did hear that they found only a hand in a black glove. Perhaps it was the hand of the pilot of the aircraft that I shot down. You know, even now I cannot really believe that there were passengers on board. You cannot write off everyone to the crabs . . . Surely something would be left? . . . Nevertheless, I am a supporter of the old version: It was a spy plane. In any event, it was not happenstance that it flew towards us."[75]

Professor William Newman, marine biologist, explains why the crab (or any other sea creature) theory is untenable:

> "Even if we proceed from the supposition that crusta-
> ceans, or sharks, or something else fell upon the flesh, the
> skeletons should have remained. In many cases, skeletons were
> found on the sea or ocean floor, which had sat there for many
> years and even decades. In addition, the crustaceans would not
> have touched bones."[76]

The fourth explanation is provided us by *Izvestiya* correspondents Shalnev and Illesh through the mouth of Mikhail Igorevich, Captain of the *Tinro 2* submersible, interviewed for the *Izvestiya* series of articles on KAL 007. In the May 31, 1991 edition, Igorevich provides this fourth explanation—the passengers were sucked out of the air-

[75] Izvestiya, February 8, 1991, p. 7.

[76] ibid.

craft, leaving their clothes behind! Igorevich's words are included to demonstrate how esoteric the theories become when once the simple conclusion that the passengers were rescued is precluded. Igorevich, nevertheless, provides unintended support for the contention of passenger rescue by the very information he supplies to illustrate the paucity of passenger remains.

"Something else was inexplicable to us—zipped up clothes. For instance, a coat, slacks, shorts, a sweater with zippers—the items were different, but, zipped up. And nothing inside. We came to this conclusion then: Most likely, the passengers had been pulled out of the plane by decompression, and they fell in a completely different place from where we found the debris. They had been spread out over a much larger area. The current also did its work."[77]

Needless to say, this "much larger area" has never been located!

In such ways do our feverish imaginations work when we close our eyes to the truth staring us in the face! But the underlying current in all these theories is the irrepressible need to explain or explain away one salient fact—there ought to have been bodies but there were not!

The mysterious disappearance of the passengers' and crew's bodies, as well as the nonappearance of luggage (or any other cargo area item) among the 1,020 fragments of flotsam and debris which were retrieved, will be further discussed in a later chapter. But with this chronicle of KAL 007's post-hit flight, we may now complete the list of indicators supporting the contention that KAL 007 was under a "good measure" of controllability during its entire post-missile impact flight. The entire list reads as follows:

- Sufficient oxygen for pilot alertness.

- All engines were operating normally.

---

[77] Izvestiya, May 28, 1991, p. 8.

- Electrical system was operative. (Otherwise, the plane's radio and engines would not have operated).

- Demonstrated pilot ability to decrease speed of KAL 007 in its downward phase. (If he would not have been able to do so, the aircraft would continue to increase its downward acceleration—only to collide with the water in from 2 to 2-1/2 minutes. KAL 007's flight lasted at least 12 minutes).

- KAL 007 was able to regain its pre-missile hit altitude almost exactly. (It is highly unlikely that KAL 007 regained exact altitude after its arc by chance.)

- KAL 007 was able to regain its pre-missile hit rate of forward acceleration.

- Captain Chun was able to bring KAL 007's nose (pitch) to the plane's exact level of flight.

- KAL 007 was able to maneuver turns.

- Captain and/or crew were able to occupy themselves with preparing the passengers for emergency sea landing and rescue.

- KAL 007 was able to descend in spirals and/or was able to circle.

CHAPTER 4

In the Water

1991—Tiberius, Israel

Climbing the steps to the second floor of the hostel at the Sea of Galilee, Exie and I could already hear the familiar strains of the congregational singing. Inside the air-conditioned meeting room, though, the unusual awaited us. The congregation was composed of new Russian immigrants to Israel, Jews and non-Jews—or Jewish men or women with their Gentile spouses. They were now new Israelis. Many of them had been accomplished in their fields in their former country. In Russia they had been musicians, doctors, and engineers; in Israel, they were making beds in lakeside hotels, mopping floors in restaurants, and collecting entrance shekels at public restrooms. Their pastor was a former "kibbutznik," preaching in Hebrew. His sermon was being translated into Russian by a young woman soldier, herself a new immigrant to Israel.

Exie and I were also asked to speak to the congregation. Afterwards, as I had become accustomed to doing, I spoke about KAL 007, hoping that someone from among these new immigrants had heard something, seen something, that could give us a new lead.

That day it happened. A middle-aged, bespeckled immigrant rushed towards us at the conclusion of our talk, speaking excitedly in Russian. With the help of the translator, we heard his story. A few years previous, when he was still in Murmansk, a friend of his had shown him a photograph. This friend had been one of the Murmansk divers and the photograph showed KAL 007 under water and resting on the bottom. It showed a fuselage with holes in it, but otherwise intact.

This encounter at Tiberius had occurred before we had heard about the Izvestiya series, before disclosure of the CIA report, before Boris Yeltsin had handed over the black box tapes, before the issuance of the 1993 ICAO report. But just in time to give us the push forward, the assurance that we were on the right track.

The Surface Finds

A few hours after KAL 007 was downed, Tommy Toles, the press aid of Congressman Larry McDonald, received two messages in his Georgia office. One was from C.K. Suh, the manager of the Los Angeles Korean Airlines regional office. Suh told Toles that Korean Airlines in Seoul had reported that the U.S. Embassy in Korea had informed the Korean Ministry of Foreign Affairs that, "the plane landed in Sakhalin." The second message came from Federal Aviation Agency (FAA) Washington-based spokesman Orville Brockman. He reported that the FAA representative in Tokyo, Dennis Wilham, had been advised by the Japanese Civil Aviation Bureau (the FAA's Japanese counterpart) that, "Japanese Self-Defense Force confirms that the Hokkaido radar followed Air Korea to a landing in Soviet territory on the island of Sakhalinska—S-a-k-h-a-l-i-n-s-k-a. And it confirmed by the manifest that Congressman McDonald is on board." Based on this information, commentator Robert W. Lee concluded that since KAL 007 was flying away from Sakhalin after it had been rocketed, it must have made a 180 degree turn in order for it to be followed by Hokkaido radar "to a landing in Soviet territory on the island of Sakhalinska." Lee furthermore concluded that KAL 007 had, indeed, landed on the island itself! But, granted the 180 degree turn, KAL 007 might just as well have landed in the Tatar Straits, in waters between Sakhalin and Moneron Islands, rather than on the island itself.

Most commentators have indeed concluded that KAL 007 did land in the water and that the water landing was "in pieces"—due to either a midair explosion, a high-speed collision with the sea, or both. But there is another possibility—KAL 007 made a successful water landing, after which all or most of the passengers and crew were evacuated from the airliner, which was then sunk and exploded under the sea in order to cover Soviet culpability for the shoot-down.

In order to evaluate these possibilities, we need to understand the "egalitarian" characteristic of midair explosions or plane crashes at sea. The sinking of the "unsinkable" Titanic was decidedly un-egalitarian. 1,513 lives were lost when the Titanic went down; only 700 survived. All the children in First Class, except one, were saved, while 49 children in Steerage perished. The overall survival rates were as follows: 63% of first class passengers, 47% of second class passengers, and 25% of third class passengers. This was primarily due to the location of these passenger groups in the hull of the ship at the time it struck the iceberg, but "class structure" prejudices played their parts as well.

Many commentators believe that a crash on land of an aircraft is likewise discriminatory, though to a lesser degree. Often enough, the tail section is shorn away with great structural damage, and consequently greater loss of life to the passengers seated to the rear of the fuselage than to those seated in the mid-or fore section of the aircraft. Other commentators deny this structural "bias."

But no other term than "egalitarian" can be used in cases of midair explosions or plane crashes at sea. In these instances, almost immediately after the crash or midair explosion, there is an indiscriminate mixture of flotsam and debris at the crash site. This admixture is made up of bodies; various articles which were with or on the persons of the passengers; articles from the cabin itself such as sweaters, jackets, dinner trays, life vests, magazines; articles from the cargo section of the aircraft such as suitcases, packing crates, cartons, sporting goods, industrial and electronic equipment; and finally, various sized fragments of the aircraft itself. The greater the altitude of the aircraft at the time of the explosion, or the greater the duration of breakup and disintegration in the air—even at lower altitudes—the more scattered and diffuse the flotsam and debris turned out. It is virtually impossible for there to be a midair explosion and subsequent crash at sea without these features obtaining.

But they did not obtain in the case of KAL 007. To understand this further, we need to compare the immediate resultant aftermaths of actual crashes having similar conditions to the alleged crash of KAL 007 with the case of KAL 007 itself.[78]

Case One. Air India Boeing 747 Flight 182 was blown up by a terrorist bomb while flying above the North Atlantic near the coast of Ireland on June 23, 1985. It was then at the altitude of 31,000 feet, about 4,000 feet less than that of KAL 007 when it was hit. Flight 182 plunged into the sea, killing all 329 passengers and crew. That same day, 123 bodies were recovered, and the next day eight more were recovered. Four months later, another body was recovered, strapped to its seat in a section of the fuselage lifted from the ocean bottom. The bodies were described by British Royal Navy doctor, Lt. Richard Cribb as "badly shattered and broken but all in one piece."[79]Over 40 percent of the passengers of Flight 182 were recovered, and from a depth of about 6,700 feet beneath the ocean surface. Debris was dispersed across four miles of sea bottom, and for a month luggage and other debris could be seen floating on the Irish Sea. Search operations had lasted four months.

Case Two. A South African Airlines Boeing 747 crashed into the Indian Ocean on November 28, 1987. Aircraft debris, luggage, and bodies were scattered over 150 square miles and to the great depth of 12,000 feet. At least 15 of the 159 passenger and crew bodies were recovered—that is, about ten percent. Much luggage and debris were seen floating on the ocean surface for days. The search continued for one year.

Case Three. On July 3, 1988, during Operation Earnest Will, over 200 people were killed when the U.S.S. Vincennes, an Aegis class cruiser, shot down an Iranian Airbus passenger plane over the Persian Gulf toward the conclusion of the Iraq-Iran War. Hundreds

---

[78] Prior to the downing of KAL 007 on September 1, 1983, a Boeing 747 had never crashed at sea, making it more difficult for investigators and general public alike to imagine what the aftermath might be.

[79] A. P. dispatch, Deseret News, June 24, 1985.

of intermingled bodies and pieces of luggage were retrieved from the water.

Case Four. On January 28, 1986, at a height of 38,000 feet—3000 feet higher than KAL 007 when it was rocketed—the Space Shuttle Challenger experienced an explosion of such magnitude that parts of the space craft were hurled to an altitude of 52,800 feet (ten miles high!). This is the largest non-nuclear explosion that has ever occurred. "Yet, despite an explosive inferno that would make a Soviet rocket detonation (involving perhaps seventy pounds of explosives, the amount of the Anab missiles of the type fired at KAL 007 contain) seem like a firecracker, searches soon recovered more than twenty tons of the challenger wreckage."[80] The bodies of all seven crew members were recovered—100% recovery rate—mangled but all identifiable.

Case Five. July 17, 1996. Trans World Airlines Flight 800, a Boeing 747, exploded due to mechanical causes in the air over the Atlantic.[81] All 230 passengers and crew perished. All 230 passengers and crew were recovered and identified over a one-year period, the last two being identified through DNA analysis.

The case of KAL 007. On September 1, 1983, rocketed at 35,000 feet over Sakhalin Island. Aircraft remains and other debris located on the surface and at shallow depths of Tatar Straits ranging from 656 feet (200 meters) to 1,640 feet (800 meters).

Luggage recovered at sites—0

Bodies recovered at sites—0

Percentage of bodies recovered—0

Amount of aircraft structural debris—"likened to that of a crash of a Piper Cub."[82]

The total amount of debris, including aircraft structural parts and

---

[80] Robert W. Lee in the "New American," August 29, 1988.

[81] The FBI's best conjecture posited the following: The central fuel tank was empty of fuel but filled with fumes. The plane had been sitting on the runway for a long period of time getting hot. Air conditioners were under the central tank heating it up. An electric cable passed over the tank. There may have been a short circuit which caused the heated fuel vapor in the tank to explode.

[82] CIA/Republican Staff Study, p. 10.

fragments of parts, passenger belongings, cabin articles, and even including the 13 unidentifiable body parts found awash eight days later at the Japanese coastline hundreds of miles from the shoot-down (of doubtful connection to the shoot-down itself)—1,020 small pieces.[83] Of this number, 785 (77%) were supplied by the Japanese and only 235 (23%) were handed over by the Soviets.

The CIA report concludes that "Almost all of KAL 007's wreckage, luggage, and all the 269 innocent people on it seem to have simply disappeared completely on the night of August 31—September 1, 1983, almost without a trace . . . The lack of debris from KAL 007, as compared to empirical evidence from other events presumed to be similar to the KAL 007 incident involving massive amounts of debris, suggests that massive amounts of debris also should have been recovered from KAL 007, if it indeed 'crashed.'[84]

"Because of the fact that there was a dearth of remains from KAL 007, and such little debris was late being recovered, it is reasonable to speculate that maybe KAL 007 did not crash after all."[85]

The United States terminated its search for KAL 007 on November 7, 1983, just one month and six days after the shoot-down. Japan terminated its search two days later. The United Nations International Civil Aviation Organization (ICAO) finished its investigation and issued its report in December of that year. All soon came to a standstill. A study of the nature of the floating debris at both the "crash site" and at the shores of Hokkaido should have alerted the governmental agencies charged responsible for the investigation that not only was the rescue of the passengers suggested by the nature of the evidence, their rescue was indeed required by it. The 1,020 items that had been recovered included dentures, newspapers, books, seat cushions, 8 "KAL" paper cups, shoes, sandals and sneakers, a camera case, a "please fasten seatbelt" sign, an oxygen mask, a handbag, blouses,

---

[83] The largest item was a 30 x 36 inch strip of metal believed to have come from the vertical tail fin.

[84] The miniscule amount of KAL 007's debris may be compared with the Challenger's 20 tons of debris (245,000 pounds) and Air India Flight 182's more than 4 tons of debris (4,480 pounds).

[85] CIA/Republican Staff Study, p. 10.

a bottle of dishwashing liquid, an identity card belonging to 25-year old passenger Mary Jane Hendrie of Sault Ste. Marie, Canada, bottles, a vest, the business card of passenger Kathy Brown-Spier of New York, and a baby doll.

All of these items, as well as all the other nonstructural items that were recovered, came from only one section of the jumbo jet—the passenger cabin, the "top section" of the aircraft which includes its distinctive hump. Nothing had been recovered and nothing had been reported floating on the ocean surface that had come from the "bottom section" of the aircraft's fuselage—the cargo hold.

This alone ought to have alerted investigators that the passenger jet could not have exploded in the air—neither at missile impact (as would nine years later be confirmed by the black box tape analysis), nor in proximity to the Japanese cuttlefish boat *Chidori Maru* (as would be confirmed nine years later by analysis of Soviet ground-to-ground communication—the explosion seen by the boat crew occurred at 6:30 a.m., while KAL 007 had been tracked by the Soviets at 6:34 a.m. flying 16,400 feet over Moneron, 22 1/2 miles distance from the *Chidori Maru*). Nor could KAL 007 have crashed at sea since such a conjectured crash at such conjectured force would also have demolished the aircraft "top and bottom." No suitcase (over 450 were on board), crate, carton, or any other cargo area item emerged from the deep.

It should have been apparent from the start that KAL 007 had successfully landed and that any explosion of the aircraft could only have occurred subsequent to its landing, and after all passengers, crew, and luggage had been removed.

The CIA/Republican Staff Study of 1991 concluded that, "The only way to explain the lack of wreckage, bodies, and luggage from this great airliner incident is to assume that after its twelve-minute flight in search of a landing spot, KAL 007 successfully ditched at sea, and that the Soviets either rescued all the passengers who survived and recovered their luggage, or that the Soviets recovered all the bodies, wreckage, and the luggage. Since the Soviets are now known to have recovered the black boxes and the wreckage, as revealed in 1991 by Izvestiya, it is reasonable to presume that the Soviets also recovered at least all the passengers, dead or alive[86], and all the luggage."[87]

"Passengers, dead or alive." But did the Soviets ever find dead passengers of this ill-fated flight? To sharpen the question—did the Soviet divers who located the remains of KAL 007 at the shallow bottom of waters of the Tatar Strait off Moneron Island find KAL 007's passengers and crew dead?

KAL 007 From Below

> "Remember that it took the downed plane about 10 minutes[88] to plunge toward the ocean. During this time, many passengers, if not all, put on their life vests. In addition, they certainly strapped themselves in with seat belts. No matter how hard the aircraft hit the water, it is difficult to imagine all 269 people disappearing without a trace. Some of the passengers should have been carried to the surface precisely by their life vests. Some should have remained at the bottom, strapped to the seats. All of them could not have disappeared."
>
> —James Oberg, former NASA official, specialist in crash analysis.

---

[86] It would have been possible to have recovered passengers alive from the water as well as from the plane. If there had not been dead bodies, there should have been live passengers floating in the water. The water temperature around Moneron Island was 50°F. Survival manuals provide the following survival rates of persons in water—provided they could swim or had some support: up to 50 minutes—almost 100% survival; up to 3 ½ hours—50%; past 3 ½ hours—acceleratingly, down to 0% survival. Since soviet Admiral Sidorov had stated that Soviet vessels were at the scene 27 minutes after KAL 007 had come down, and since there were no dead bodies floating on the water, as Admiral Sidorov had stated, there should have been, if they had not been, in reality, absconded, almost the entire complement of the jet—269 persons alive.

[87] The CIA/Republican Staff Study was written prior to Boris Yeltsin's surrender of the actual black box tapes to the ICAO in Montreal.

[88] At least 12 minutes according to combined Soviet/Japanese radar trackings.

Not having the benefit of learning what subsequent Boeing 747 explosions and crashes at sea would provide (KAL 007 was the first Boeing 747 to allegedly explode and crash into the sea), and being convinced that KAL 007 had "cataclysmically" and "catastrophically" been "destroyed" in the air and had "cartwheeled," "hurled earthward," "whirled," "plunged," and "free-fallen" with "ever-increasing acceleration"[89] to its doom, many commentators have concluded that 269 corpses could be found incarcerated in a portion or portions of KAL 007's fuselage, their underwater tomb.

Then a bomb shell went off, but almost inaudibly—deadened, as it were, as terrorist bombs are deadened when they are exploded before their time in the remote-controlled, steel-jawed containers of a bomb squad. The bomb shell came in the form of a series of articles, part interview, part analysis, published in the Soviet newspaper *Izvestiya* from December 1990 through June 1991, the subject of which was the KAL 007 shoot-down. The dulling and deadening container of the bomb shell's blast was that investigators and the media soon realized that these articles had been published by a not-yet-free opinion-forming organ of the Communist regime, and was being used by the Soviets for disinformation purposes. Those among the general public who had been following events soon lost interest.

The genius of disinformation is to speak the truth—but in such a way that the fuller or the more threatening aspects of the truth not surface. Lies are ancillary. But below the surface of the waters off the coast of Sakhalin somewhere near the Island of Moneron, that fuller truth lies waiting.

Three diving groups have been documented, but there are indications that other groups were involved as well. The first of the three documented groups were the military divers assigned to the naval units on Soviet Gavan on the Siberian coast, across the Tatar Straits from Sakhalin Island. These naval divers operated two manned and two unmanned submersibles from their mother ship, the *Georgi Kozmin*.

---

[89] Oft-repeated popular media characterization for KAL 007's post-hit flight. See Appendix A for an explanation of the media's initial propensity for such descriptions.

Second, there was the Murmansk group working from the Ministry of Oil drilling ship *Mikhail Mirchink*. The *Mirchink* was a Swedish-built ship that had the great advantage of being able to coordinate its position and then dynamically stabilize its position regardless of changing wind and water conditions, without the use of anchors. This ship was of central importance in recovering most of the debris from what was probably the main location of the downed, sunk, and exploded aircraft.

The third group was the Svestapol group operating from the combined search and fishing boat, the *Hydronaut*. The *Hydronaut* was mother vessel to two small two-man submersibles, the *Tinro 2* and the *Okeanolog*. Mikhail Igorevich Girs was the designer and captain of the *Tinro 2*, the submersible used most extensively by the Svestapol divers. The *Okeanolog* made only two dives.

Admiral Vladimir Vasilyevich Sidorov, Commander of the Soviet Pacific Fleet, directed the Soviet Salvage operations, having the civilian divers as well as the military under his direct command. Chief diver for the Murmansk group, but also involved with the Svestapol team, was Vladimir Vasilyevich Zakharchenko.[90] He chronicled the diving sessions.

The Svestapol group began diving on September 15, sometime after the military divers had descended. How much earlier the military had started its work is unknown—unknown, that is, as far as the *Izvestiya* series is concerned. However, according to reports of Soviet immigrants to Israel and elsewhere, referred to in the CIA/Republican Staff Study, it was immediately after being downed—and after Soviet Coast Guard ships under the command of KGB General Romanenko had removed passengers and luggage—that KAL 007 was "towed to Soviet territorial waters near Moneron, and deliberately sunk in shallow waters inside Soviet territorial limits."[91] It would have been possible, therefore, for Soviet military divers to have commenced their diving on September 1, the very day KAL 007 was shot-down.

---

[90] Vladimir Vasilyevich Zakharchenko, not to be confused with Admiral Vladimir Vasilyevich Sidorov.

[91] CIA/Republican Staff Study report, p. 75.

The civilian divers knew that military divers had preceded them and understood, or were given to understand, that they (the civilian divers) were required because of their superior equipment.

As A. S. Torchinov, Chief of the Far Eastern Deep Water Drilling Administration and former KAL 007 "Murmansk Group" diver expresses it, "As for the divers, the military, of course, has its own underwater rescue service. But its maximum depth is 160 meters. And with the equipment the armed forces has cannot stay underwater for more than 15—20 minutes. And, judging from everything, the work takes a long time.

"So, having decided that they could not do the job with their own forces, the people in uniform began to recruit everyone they could into the search area." The explanation that civilian divers were called in because the military divers had inadequate equipment seems plausible on the surface as the militaries of a number of countries invest neither manpower nor finances adequate for the relatively rare occurrences of deep water search and salvage. For example, Israel had hired an American company, "Nauticus," which succeeded in April of 1999 in locating its long lost submarine, "Dakar," and has once again turned to Nauticus to locate wreckage and the "black boxes" of an F-16 that crashed and sank beneath the waters of the Mediterranean thirty kilometers west of Atlit on March 28, 2000. This civilian firm, Nauticus, has, to date, located for the various militaries of the world a total of twenty F-14s, F-15s and F-16s.

Yet, however plausible the explanation appears, the reports of KAL 007's Soviet civilian divers suggests that the military equipment was, indeed, adequate for the task. But, that the task they accomplished was other than the task assigned to the civilian crews. The ensuing evidence of the Soviet civilian divers suggests that the task of the military vessels—and civilian vessels commandeered by the military—was, as strange as it may seem, primarily towing then sinking the downed airliner, and then exploding the now submerged airliner and dispersing its wreckage in order to simulate an aerial explosion which civilian divers could then be called to authenticate and corroborate. And so, the Soviet Union would escape incrimination.

Here then are the main findings of both military and civilian divers. The plane as viewed and searched by the military divers was basically integral and more in one piece—more structurally sound— than when the plane was later visited by the civilian divers. The description of the plane by the military divers as being "enterable" was so at variance with the plane as viewed later by the civilian divers that Captain Mikhail Igorevich Girs, Commander of the *Tinro 2* submersible, doubts their report.[92]

"It was during one of these exchanges that we met the military divers.

"An entry in Captain Girs' diary: 'During the day, spent some time with the rescue divers. They clarified a lot of things, but it looks like our work is not over yet. They found the fuselage, closer to the tail, and there are many remains there. It was standing vertically between the reefs. They first lowered it down, and then got inside.'

"'To be honest,' continued Mikhail Igorevich, 'I did not completely believe those divers. According to them, they found the tail part of the aircraft standing upright. But this is a very large fragment of the Boeing. They said that they found it in the reefs. I also went to the reefs, but there, too, I saw only small fragments—but they were everywhere. The biggest parts I encountered were the chassis, wheels, engines, and pieces of the aircraft body.'

Yet when questioning high ranking officers at Sokol Airbase on Sakhalin Island, correspondent Andrey Illesh found confirmation that at an early stage KAL 007 was integral enough to be climbed on.

"Specialists—navy men—had found the giant aircraft in the Sea of Japan. In addition, submariners (military also) had gone to the bottom and had 'clambered' all over KAL 007 top to bottom."[93]

---

[92] *Izvestiya*, May 28, 1991, p. 8.

[93] *Izvestiya*, December 21, 1990, p. 12.

The military and civilian diving sessions at no time overlapped. When the Military divers had concluded their work, the civilian divers began. The first of the civilian divers to descend were from the Svestapol group.

"The people from Svestapol told us that they had also been working at the bottom of the Sea of Japan. On top of that, even earlier than the divers from Murmansk!"[94]

Diver Viyacheslav Popov informs us of the military's prior work, and then in amazement he informs us of a reversal in procedures—a reversal that should not have occurred.

"The first submergence was on 15 September, two weeks after the aircraft had been shot down. As we learned then, before us the trawlers had done some 'work' in the designated quadrant. It is hard to understand what sense the military saw in the trawling operation. First drag everything haphazardly around the bottom by the trawls, and then send in the submersibles? . . . It is clear that things should have been done in the reverse order."[95]

But this "reversal" supports the contention that KAL 007's final resting place was not its original placement, but that while still afloat, it had been towed from its original landing site and then sunk (and exploded); and then its wreckage dispersed to make it appear that a plane in disintegration had scattered its parts as it hurled earthward. Captain Girs confirms this general impression of secondary placement: "The impression is that all of this has been dragged here by trawl rather than falling down from the sky."[96]

By the end of September, the Soviet drilling ship *Mikhail Mirchink*, which possibly had been stationed and working east of Moneron off of Sakhalin Island, situated itself north of Moneron. Both civilian diving groups inspected, photographed, and recovered wreckage and debris from the Boeing 747. A full understanding of the fate of the 269 people requires a familiarity and appreciation of what these divers saw and—just as importantly—what they did not see. Their reactions to their underwater experience is equally informative, revealing both

---

[94] *Izvestiya*, May 27, 1991, p. 6.

[95] ibid.

[96] *Izvestiya*, May 28, 1991, p. 8.

their expectations and the minds of those who prepared them for their underwater task. For these reasons, it is best to hear their descriptions and experiences from the watery environs, as reported in *Izvestiya*.

> Viyacheslav Popov:
>
> "I will confess that we felt great relief when we found out that there were no bodies at the bottom. Not only no bodies; there were also no suitcases or large bags. Sometimes the thought even occurred: Was it really a passenger plane, or is that a deception? I remember we put together this independent version (we had to explain the situation to ourselves somehow): they did have an accident with a specific Boeing somewhere out there, but then they 'covered' it with this forgery—this spy plane."[97]

> Vladimir Bondarev:
>
> "'I discovered this human hand,' he extends a horrifying photo toward us [*Izvestiya's* reporters], 'during the second or third submergence—between 17 and 20 September. When I saw it, I decided to make sure that it was not a plaster cast—I asked the captain to zoom in on it. That was the only way to make sure that it could not be a fake.'"[98]

> Captain Mikhail Igorevich Girs:
>
> "From Captain Girs' diary: 'Submergence 10 October. Aircraft pieces, wing spars, pieces of aircraft skin, wiring, and clothing. But—no people. The impression is that all of this has been dragged here by a trawl rather than falling down from the sky . . .'"[99]
>
> "So we were ready to encounter a virtual cemetery. But one submergence went by, then the second, and then the third . . . During the entire rather lengthy period of our work

---

[97] *Izvestiya*, May 27, 1991, p. 6.

[98] Ibid.

[99] *Izvestiya*, May 28, 1991, p. 8.

near Moneron, I and my people had maybe ten encounters with the remains of Boeing passengers. No more than that."[100]

Something else was inexplicable to us—zipped up clothes. For instance, a coat, slacks, shorts, a sweater with zippers—the items were different, but— zipped up and nothing inside. We came to this conclusion then: Most likely, the passengers had been pulled out of the plane by decompression and they fell in a completely different place from where we found the debris. They had been spread out over a much larger area. The current also did its work."

V. Zakharchenko, G. Matyevenko, V. Kondrabayev:

"We thought we would go down and see a cemetery . . . But . . . There were no bodies the first day or the next . . . We learned our way around. And when I saw some remains for the first time I was surprised but not frightened. And then we did find some bones. Two . . . I took them in my hand . . . Later I saw some human skin with hair, like a scalp. The hair was black . . . But when it was touched all this fell apart . . . I saw what I thought was a fist in a glove. And then, remember, we saw a torso without a head, wearing a jacket. And winding their way out from under the jacket were some white strands—apparently the remains of entrails . . ."[101]

"I did not miss a single dive. I have quite a clear impression: The aircraft was filled with garbage, but there were really no people there. Why? Usually when an aircraft crashes, even a small one . . . As a rule there are suitcases and bags, or at least the handles of the suitcases."[102]

---

[100] There is no way of ascertaining from this testimony if the "ten encounters" were with ten separate bodies or (more likely) ten encounters with a lesser number of bodies. It is entirely possible that these encounters were with fragments from the same individual.

[101] In all the divers' reports, this is the only reference to a torso—that is, a body.

[102] "World Wide Issues," February 6, 1991, p. 21.

V. Zakharchenko:

"But the main thing was not what we had seen there but what we had not seen—the divers had found practically no human bodies or remains . . ."[103]

"Well, we found some pants with holes in the knees, a belt—also torn, everything else intact. What does this say? A person was probably wearing these pants . . . Then when we returned to Murmansk, we started reading the newspapers—we found what they were writing especially interesting. I thought at that time—it is impossible to simulate the death of such a number of people . . . to organize their relatives who would be in mourning—in Korea, Thailand, the United States, Taiwan . . . You might be able to fake two or three—but two hundred or more? . . ."[104]

"But there was no fire in the Boeing—that is for sure. Things were intact, although all thoroughly saturated with kerosene. So . . . you heard all kinds of talk among members of this expedition—like there were no people there, on this aircraft, that all this was a falsification. All in all, I too was of this opinion at first. Almost no traces indicating people there, except for personal effects. But there were personal effects! Judging from the clothing, clothing worn by people. Why? Because it was torn. The way I see it—the people were cut apart by fragments."

"No, they were not looking for people at all. They were looking for something they feared more than the tears and the curses of those who lost their loved ones . . ."

"No, no one asked us to recover people's remains. Only—components, tapes, documents, the black box."[105]

Based on the facts presented in this and in the previous chapter, we can now list the evidence for the successful rescue by the Soviets of at least 259 of the 269[106] passengers of KAL 007.

---

[103] ibid., p. 19.

[104] ibid., p. 20.

[105] ibid., p. 21.

[106] The ten passenger disparity takes into account the unlikely possibility that the

- Within 27 minutes of KAL 007's landing on water, small Soviet craft were at the site—Admiral Sidorov.

- Contrary to all known passenger plane explosions in air/ crashes at sea, bodies were not found floating on the surface of the sea.

- Contrary to all known passenger plane explosions in air/ crashes at sea, suitcases were not found floating on the sea (KAL 007 would have carried over 450 suitcases in the cargo area).

- Contrary to all known passenger plane explosions in air/ crashes at sea, and contrary to the egalitarian nature of midair explosions/crashes at sea, not one item of the 1,020 items recovered came from KAL 007's cargo area.

- There is evidence that KAL 007, or portions of it, may have been moved under the sea by the first diving team, that of the military, and by trawls, and then scattered in order to simulate crash debris dispersal.

- Contrary to what should have obtained in an aircraft explosion in the air, no aircraft wreckage recovered and no wreckage viewed under the sea by the divers evidenced burn marks.

- KAL 007 was viewed more or less intact under the water by the first diving team, the military divers.

- At an early stage, the military divers describe the fuselage as intact enough to be entered and even climbed upon "top to bottom."

---

divers' ten encounters with the remains of Boeing passengers were with the remains of ten separate individuals.

- At a later stage, the civilian divers describe KAL 007 as being in pieces and fragments. This could only have occurred if there had been an underwater explosion.[107]

- Divers report with astonishment the absence of bodies on board or in association with the sunken airliner. (But one diver reports seeing one decapitated torso—while not more than ten "encounters" with body fragments are noted throughout all of divers' reports.)

- Divers report with astonishment the absence of luggage aboard or in association with the sunken airliner. (But one diver reports seeing some suitcases.)

- Some civilian divers express astonishment that they had not been briefed concerning passengers' bodies, whereas they had been briefed concerning the black box and electronic equipment locations.

- The contention of the Soviet divers, as well as Admiral Sidorov, that there were no bodies found could not have been contrived to support the initial Soviet position that KAL 007 was a spy plane without civilians, as General Ogarkov had years previous—on September 9, 1983—conceded that KAL 007 was a passenger plane carrying civilian passengers which the United States had cynically used for espionage purposes. All evidence, therefore, suggests the sincerity of the Russian divers' claims that there were no bodies aboard or in association with the sunken airliner.

---

[107] See earlier. The disparity between the few and tiny fragments actually handed over by the Soviets and reported by the Soviet divers, and a basically intact aircraft that would be entered as reported by some divers and military sources to Isvestia, is truly striking.

CHAPTER 5

Rescue, Cover-up and Aftermath

When considering the possibility of KAL 007's passengers and crew having been rescued after a successful water ditching, there is a great deal of congruity in the data presented to us by various sources. Whereas the possibility of "rescue" seemed unthinkable in the past, due in no small part to the Soviet concealment of their recovery of the black boxes and to their retention of ground-to-ground "shoot-down" communiqués, this situation is now reversed. With Soviet salvage divers' reports published, black box tapes deciphered, ground-to-ground communication revealed, and Russian émigré's experiences digested, it now seems highly unlikely that the passengers and crew were not rescued.

The Time Frame

As in all historical reconstruction, we need to set the time frame for consideration—to bracket out those events which appear to have a bearing but which are, in reality, irrelevant. We have already excluded the explosion close to the water at 6:30 a.m. witnessed and heard by the crew of the Japanese cuttlefish boat, the *Chidori Maru*, on the grounds that it could not have been of KAL 007, which had been reported at 6:34 at 16,400 feet altitude 22 1/2 miles away, slowly descending over Moneron Island.

We now need to bracket out a certain KGB patrol boat commanded by a Captain Anisimov. The KGB, under the general command of General Romanenko, exercised general surveillance duties in the waters off Sakhalin Island. In the early predawn hours of August 31-September 1, 1983, Captain Anisimov's patrol boat had been cruising the waters north of Moneron, not far from where the *Chidori Maru* crew had seen something explode.[108] Anisimov was interviewed in 1991 by the Japanese newspaper *Daily Yomiuri*, which reported that

> "Valeri Anisimov, Captain of the Soviet Frontier Guard, described how he had detected the approaching jetliner on radar while he was on duty in a patrol boat off Nevelsk.
>
> "He said that he detected a bright dot on the radar at around 3:23 a.m. [6:23 Sakhalin time], which was moving at about 800 km/h. He said it split into two then three pieces before vanishing. The plane apparently split into three sections before falling into the sea, Anisimov said."[109]

In this account, a disintegrating aircraft was viewed by Anisimov on his radar at 6:23—11 minutes prior to an intact and flying KAL 007 being located around 22 1/2 miles away over Moneron Island.[110] This might have been the exploding aircraft sighted by the *Chidori Maru*, but the descriptions are somewhat different from each other. Whereas the *Chidori Maru* sighting involved a plane (apparently) which exploded upon or near impact with the sea, the patrol boat radar sighting was of a plane breaking up and fragmenting successively into three sections.[111] In any case, we can now rule out the Anisimov sighting as being irrelevant, for the same reason that those of the *Chidori Maru* were—KAL 007 was pinpointed independently by both radar and the more recently published (1993) Soviet

---

[108] The *Chidori Maru*, No. 58, was located at coordinates 46°35'N, 141°16'E at the time of its sighting. Anisimov's radar sighting locates an exploding aircraft at a slight distance away at coordinates 46°33'N, 141°18'E.

[109] The *Daily Yomiuri*, August 12, 1991, p. 2.

[110] Another version has Anisimov's sighting at 6:32—two minutes prior to an intact and flying KAL 007 being sighted 22 1/2 miles away.

[111] Michel Brun contends that the one blip breaking up into, successively, three blips was not an aircraft breaking up, but rather the "peeling off" of three aircraft in classic attack formation. This contention, of course, supports the air battle/mini-war understanding of the KAL incident.

communiqués as stricken but under control and flying at 16,400 feet altitude, miles away and minutes after.

But all this leaves us with the astounding thought—the shoot-down of KAL 007, far from being an isolated incident involving a straying aircraft, was part of a larger and more ominous scenario in which an air battle had taken place during which perhaps both Russian and American planes had been shot down. A "mini-war" had occurred which both sides have concealed. Evidence for this battle has been marshaled by Michel Brun,[112] including the following description of debris recovered north of Moneron Island by the Japanese Maritime Safety Agency within three days of the shoot-down:

- Part of the wing flaps from the United States two seat electronic warfare fighter EF-111.

- Pilot's ejection seat shell, identical with, or similar to, the McDonnell Douglas Aces II Zero Zero ejection seat. The propulsive charges were fired indicating that the seat had been used.

- Part of the tail fin of a non-Soviet infrared guided heat seeking missile. ("N3" is marked on the fin. "N" does not appear in the Cyrillic alphabet and so it appears that the fin is not "Soviet block.")[113]

On the other end of the time frame, we may mark 3 1/2 hours after the shooting down of KAL 007. It was at that time (10 a.m. Sakhalin time), that the Soviet trawler *Uvarovsk* spotted and began

---

[112] Incident at Sakhalin: The True Mission of KAL Flight 007, Michel Brun, Four Walls Eight Windows, New York, 1995).

[113] Japanese Maritime Safety Agency report dated September 5, 1983. The Agency photographed, tagged, and recorded the finds. Brun, with his body of specialists, has made the identifications—at least in one case with significant divergence from JMSA identification. According to Brun, the tail fin mentioned above had been erroneously identified by the JMSA as the aileron of a light civilian plane.

retrieving floating debris belonging, as we have seen, exclusively to KAL 007's passenger compartment. According to the *Izvestiya* series[114] and the Japanese newspaper *Yomiuri Shimbun*,[115] Captain Ivan Bilyuk, commanding the Soviet trawler and fishing boat *Uvarovsk* on its return to the port of Korsakov on the southern coast of Sakhalin Island, received orders to proceed west of Moneron and "to remain on the lookout for any objects or persons floating on the surface of the water." Having found nothing there, Bilyuk was ordered to proceed north of Moneron, where he found the debris—but no bodies. The Soviet trawler *Zabaikalye*, the largest out of the port of Nevelsk and commanded by Captain Vladimir Alexeiv, continued the task of recovering the debris after the *Uvarovsk* left the crash sight.

If we were to accept the ultimately Soviet "only" authenticated time of 10:00am[116] for the arrival of the *Uvarovsk* on the scene[117], we would have thus a time framework of 3 1/2 hours within which to fit all the pieces of our puzzle providing us with a composite picture of the following:

- A successful ditching of the disabled airliner.

- An evacuation of at least 259 of the 269 passengers and crew to awaiting Soviet patrol boats as well as possible other vessels.

- The transferring of passenger luggage to awaiting Soviet patrol boats as well as possible other vessels.

---

[114] October 15, 1991.

[115] October 17, 1991.

[116] 10:00am turns out to be a significant time for "disclosure." It was at 10:00am (Korean time) that the relatives of the KAL 007 passengers lost all hope of an eventual safe landing at Kimpo Airport. Flight 007's fuel reserve received at Anchorage, Alaska would be used up by that time.

[117] The Soviet fixing of the time at 10:00am is accepted here and it is quite possibly accurate. We need note here only that the Soviet fixing of the *Uvarovsk's* arrival might well have been self-serving, verification or non-verification has come from no other quarter.

- The commencement of transport of passengers, crew, and luggage to the Soviet Gavan mainland.

- The removal of the black boxes and other related electronic control equipment.

- The towing of the empty aircraft to another location.

- The sinking, underwater photographing, and exploding of the sunken aircraft in order to simulate an aircraft which had exploded in the air and had crashed in the sea.

As we shall see, most of these elements could be and were accomplished simultaneously and all were concluded well within the 3 1/2 hour "window of opportunity." We must remember that though the terminus of the time frame was the arrival of the *Uvarovsk*, the *Uvarovsk* itself was but another pawn in the hands of the Soviets, and could well have been *so very timely* directed to the "crash" scene only after the airplane had been destroyed underwater. Thus the real determiner of the terminus might well have been the escalating joint United States, Japanese, and Korean search and salvage operations which threatened to bring disclosure in their wake.

A New Source

In November of 1990, Avraham Shifrin's work—including signed testimonies, original protocols, and interviews all relating to the successful ditching at sea of KAL Flight 007 and the rescue of its passengers and crew—was communicated to U.S. Senator Jesse Helms, chairman of the United States Senate Committee on Foreign Relations and passenger on Korean Airlines flight 015, KAL 007's accompanying sister flight on that fateful night. Helms, in response, sent then Minority Staff Director of his Committee, Dr. James Lucier, and two other staff assistants, David Sullivan and V. Fedei, to Israel to receive the complete and detailed results of the Shifrin investigation.

For a fascinating insight into the development of knowledge and operation of the powerful Senate Committee on Foreign Relations, these results were published in the January 16, 1991, summary of Staff Assistant David Sullivan to Committee Chairman Senator Helms.

"SUMMARY: The world's leading expert on the Soviet Gulag prison system has suggested that he has access to and can obtain further credible evidence that most of the passengers on KAL 007 survived the August 31—September 1, 1983 incident, and have been held prisoner in secret Soviet Gulag concentration camps for foreigners along the Sino-Soviet border near ___.[118] If this information can be confirmed, it could change the course of U.S.-Soviet relations. He also provided information that the CIA and the State Department were penetrated by Soviet moles in the early 1950s.

"While I was in Israel, I was instructed to meet with Avraham Shifrin, a Russian Jewish émigré who went to Israel in 1970. Shifrin is the world's leading expert on the Soviet Gulag prison system, and we cited his writings and maps in your 1988 INF Red Book.[119]

"Avraham Shifrin provided the following new information:

"KAL 007 was damaged but not shot down, and it was forced to land on Sakhalin Island. Most of the passengers survived, and are still being held prisoner at three secret Soviet Gulag prison camps expressly used for foreign prisoners near___[120] along the Sino-Soviet border. These camps are located near ___ ___, ___ ___, and ___.[121]

"KAL 007 was searched and stripped of its "Black Box" and all navigation and electronic equipment and luggage. The Soviet

---

[118] Deleted by present author.

[119] Shifrin had already, in 1983, presented testimony on U.S.S.R. labor camps before the Judiciary's Sub-Committee to Investigate the Administration of the Internal Security Act and Other Internal Security Laws. (ISBN: 088264159X)

[120] Deleted by present author.

[121] ibid.

military and KGB were trying to prove that it was on a spy mission, but they could find no evidence. A special, secret KGB-GRU commission was set up to control this entire operation, by the highest level of the Soviet government. KAL 007 was then taken to waters of about 100 meters depth near Sakhalin, and deliberately sunk. Soviet scuba divers who were not part of the commission were sent to investigate and photograph the largely intact 'wreck.' U.S. Navy ships and divers also observed the Soviet divers and 'wreck,' but this was never made public.

"Three sources reported the above information to Shifrin. One source, a top KGB official who wants to defect to the U.S., wrote a letter to Shifrin in June, 1990, containing the names of top KGB-GRU Soviet Generals and Colonels and institutes involved in the secret KAL 007 commission. This source does not trust the U.S. government, and wants assistance for his defection. Another source is a top Soviet criminal, who has verified some of the above information, and will provide and corroborate further information for money. The third source is a high ranking Soviet scientist who is already in the United States on a scientific exchange program."

After the findings and results of Shifrin's investigation were conveyed to Helms, the Senator asked the CIA to initiate its own study. Completed in June, 1991, the CIA study was first leaked and then publicized by its title page and inner reference of page 43, "Top Secret/Codeword CIA Republican Staff Study." It was this document that was first publicly disclosed in the South Korean parliament in October of 1992 by Korean legislator and opposition leader Sonn Se-Il, and published in part by Reuters News Service on October 26, 1992.[122]

---

[122] That Shifrin's research forms the basis, at least in part, for the CIA study is evident in the final section of the report, which refers to émigré reports of the Soviet radar tracking in almost the exact words of Shifrin's previously published reports. This, of course, was proper, as the CIA report here has concluded its analysis and is merely conveying testimony.

The second page summary of this document was published in the Issues and Trends section of the Korean language *Win* magazine of January 2, 1996—the second of a planned multipart serial on KAL 007. The Korean CIA forbade further publication of this series after this issue and prevented further media contact in Israel regarding flight 007. That Shifrin's material was the catalyst for the CIA report, and that the CIA had confirmed at least part of Shifrin's findings, is confirmed by United States Navy Rear Admiral (retired) Bud Nance, who had replaced James Lucier on Helms' committee as Minority Staff Director. In Admiral Nance's letter to Shifrin of February 11, 1992, he stated, "The information which you conveyed to them last year is safe and protected as David [Sullivan] told you, a copy of it was given to the Central Intelligence Agency for possible corroboration. The CIA found your information very interesting and consistent with some of their information . . .

"Enclosed are copies of two letters[123] to Russian president Boris Yeltsin which Senator Helms sent in December. You can see that the

---

[123] The second letter sent by Helms to Yeltsin related to the POW/MIA issue. The letter sent by Helms and 91 other congressional office holders asked Yeltsin to help facilitate retrieval of information related to reports of Soviet retention and detention of World War II, Korean, and Vietnamese era U.S. POWs and MIAs. Yeltsin responded to this letter, as well as to increasing pressure from other sources, by an amazing statement six months later, and by authorizing joint U.S./Soviet search operations in certain areas of the former Soviet Union. Yeltsin's startling statement was made on June 15, 1992 while being interviewed aboard his presidential jet on his way to the United States, "Our archives have shown that it is true—some of them [American POW's from the Vietnam War] were transferred to the territory of the former U.S.S.R. and were kept in labor camps. . . We can only surmise that some of them may still be alive." See Appendix D for full text of Helm's letter. See also the discussion by John M.G. Brown in Chapter Fourteen of his excellent book, <u>Moscow Bound: Policy, Politics and the POW/MIA</u> Dilemma, Veteran Press, Eureka Springs, California, 1993.

letter inquiring about the fate of KAL 007 is a direct result of your information."[124]

Helms' letter to Boris Yeltsin concerning flight 007 politely but firmly suggested that the Russians had indeed taken possession of KAL 007's black boxes, rescued passengers from the downed plane, and imprisoned Larry McDonald. He requested that Yeltsin make complete disclosure regarding disposition and locations of all passenger and crew members living or dead, hand over the black boxes to the U.S. and concluded with the suggestion that continuance of the recent positive developments in U.S.-Soviet relations might well depend upon Russian compliance with these requests.[125]

By March 24, 1992, Soviet Defense Minister Marshal Sergei Ustinov had admitted on Russian television in a 52 minute program dedicated to KAL 007 that he had ordered an all-out effort to retrieve the black boxes in order to "prevent the United States from finding them and to save the Soviet Union from a flurry of international accusations for destroying a civilian airliner."[126]

On October 14 of the same year, a delegation from the American Association For Families of KAL 007 Victims visited Moscow and received partial transcripts of Cockpit Voice Recorder and Digital Flight Data recorder tapes from the Russian Federation—but not the tapes themselves.

The following month, Boris Yeltsin handed over KAL 007's black boxes to Korean president Roh Tae-Woo at the end of the plenary session of the Korean National Assembly with this statement, "We apologize for the tragedy and are trying to settle some unsolved issues."

But, much to his chagrin and embarrassment, the black box handed over to the Korean president contained an inferior copy of the Cockpit Voice Recorder tape and no Digital Flight Recorder tape at all. Both tapes would not be handed over until January 8, 1993, to the International Civil Aviation Organization.

---

[124] Helms sent Yeltsin a letter concerning U.S. POWs and MIAs on December 5, 1991, and a letter concerning KAL 007 on December 10—just five days later!

[125] Helms' complete letter to Yeltsin is in Appendix D.

[126] The Korean Times, March 24, 1992.

Three and a Half Hours Plus

The time has come for us to now weave together the variegated strands composing the tapestry of rescue, concealment, and deceit—and if, as in all tapestries, the underside seems a confusion of colors, blurred lines and loose ends, viewing the composite from above will communicate the cogency of the whole—how be it, without beauty, without justice.

From above, then, at 5,000 meters altitude, is where we start—

With Captain Chun at the controls, and KAL 007 shuddering, the jumbo jet continued its descent, spiraling slowly down, Captain Chun seeking the most favorable spot for ditching at sea. The plane was "shuddering" because, as ICAO analysis of the KAL 007's flight data digital recorder would conclude, "Loss of [hydraulic] systems two and three would have also disabled the yaw damper system. This would account for the presence of oscillations in the lateral accelera-tion measurements and the roll attitudes from the start of the attack phase . . ."[127]

The plane was "spiraling slowly"—as witnessed and testified to by Sakhalin fisherman as reported by Izvestiya, and as indicated by Lt. Colonel Gerasimenko to General Kornukov while the Colonel was viewing his radar screen.

Gerasimenko: (6:33)
. . . altitude of target is 5,000.

Kornukov:
5,000 already?

Gerasimenko: (6:34)
Affirmative, turning left, right, apparently . . . it is descending.[128]

---

[127] ICAO report 1993, page 54, section 2.16.5. We can assume that the shuddering continued for the duration of KAL 007's post-hit flight as hydraulic systems 2 and 3 remained disabled.

[128] ICAO report 1993, p. 136. On a radar screen, a spiral descent appears as downward reoccurring right and left zags or turns.

The passengers would be hunched forward, hands clasped at the back of their heads, life vests on. Most, if not all, of them would be shoeless, having removed them in preparation for sliding down the escape chutes that would extend from the sides of the plane once in the water. By the second and last spiral (under the 5,000 meter mark) around the island, Captain Chun would have been able to ascertain the direction and configuration of the swells.[129]

Following established training procedure, Chun would have sought to set down KAL 007 with its landing gear retracted and its flaps down, its tail slightly pointed down parallel to and upon the crest of a swell, making it less likely that the plane would become swamped in the swell's trough.

He would have also released excess fuel from the aircraft's fuel tanks. This release would have prevented an explosion from occurring in the event of a crash. The empty fuel tanks, once again sealed, would additionally provide buoyancy, enabling the plane to float for an extended period of time.

The actual landing of KAL 007 on the water was not witnessed—or, if witnessed, unreported. Presuming the buoyancy provided by emptied and sealed fuel tanks, and presuming a landing on the crest of a swell, the aircraft would be in no danger of immediately sinking. Analysis of the cockpit voice recorder established that the Cabin Alert Warning sounding a full 11 seconds after missile impact, indicating that the sum total of the punctured area in the passenger cabin was only 1 3/4 square feet; the passenger cabin being above water level, there can be no certainty that KAL 007 was "shipping" water. Yet, it is reasonable to assume that the portion of the aircraft underwater—the cargo area to the rear of the plane—was likewise perforated to the

---

[129] But the best assessment of ocean surface conditions could be made at around 2,000 feet. Under this altitude, observations are deceptive, as far as the major configuration and direction of swells are concerned. At 2,000 ft., the individual swells can be seen, but swell directions are little indication of important local wind directions or forces. These latter elements, the so-called wave or chop conditions, are determined at a lower altitude and are characterized by the relative proximity of wave crests to white caps as well as the general wave irregularities.

same extent, 1 3/4 square feet. This is in view of the fact that the Soviet Anab AA-3 mid-range air-to-air missile had detonated 50 feet from the plane, most likely flinging its fragments in the general direction of KAL 007's aft, both top and bottom.

We may conclude that within a period of half an hour, Soviet vessels had surrounded the stricken plane, and that evacuation procedures were being employed for both passengers and material (including luggage and electronic control instrumentation). This conclusion is based on the following:

- Commander of the Soviet Pacific Fleet Admiral Siderov's assertion that "within 27 minutes of the crash, small Soviet craft were on the scene . . ."[130]

- The first documented Soviet rescue mission, initiated by Lt. Colonel Novoseletski, involving rescue helicopters, KGB, and border guards,[131] was ordered just nine minutes after KAL 007 had reached point zero altitude (1,000 feet) and therefore probably just six or seven minutes after it had landed on the water.

- According to émigré reports in Israel, as well as United States sources, the Soviet's arrival was "immediate." "The émigrés also report that Soviet small boats were immediately on the scene of KAL 007's ditching, which is also consistent with U. S. intelligence information."[132]

The Location of KAL 007's Landing

Here in Jerusalem, the traditional site of Jesus' crucifixion and resurrection is the Church of the Holy Sepulchre. In the fourth century,

---

[130] It is likely that "the 27 minute" figure represents a historic reality—though the Admiral purports that the plane had indeed crashed, creating debris "but no bodies." The rapid arrival of Soviet vessels was apparently not refutable.

[131] ICAO report 1993, p. 93.

[132] Top Secret/Codeword CIA report, p. 76.

the Byzantine emperor Constantine's mother Helena, doing amateur archeological work, fixed the site, learning that the pagan emperor Hadrian in the second century had tried to wipe out the memory of Christ's Great Acts by erecting a temple to Jupiter over the very spot where the Christians of his day commemorated the place of Christ's death and resurrection. Indeed, the church built by Constantine must have been an enormously difficult engineering project, due to the unevenness of Golgotha's terrain—a rock quarry outside the ancient city's walls. Apparently, Constantine felt no freedom to build in an easier but less "historical" location.

But there is another traditional Golgotha, equally probable, equally convincing— Gordon's Calvary. Discovered and excavated in the nineteenth century, it exhibits Byzantine crosses and even a proven first century "Joseph of Aramathea" rich man's garden described by the Gospel narrative, which the Holy Sepulchre does not evidence.

Holy Sepulchre or Gordon's Calvary? Which was the true place of Christ's death? Many thought an artillery shell had decided the issue. In the 1948 Israeli-Arab war, an artillery shell landed in the Dormition Abbey, King David's tomb enclosures on Mt. Zion. A small room—King David's tomb portion—was damaged. This room was located where the fifth century Byzantine Madaba map and the later Prudentia Mosaic showed an honored room—so honored that the Byzantines built the great Holy Zion Basilica Church abutting it, and the Crusaders built their Church of St. Mary over it. Almost as soon as the shell hit the room, the Israelis rushed in archaeologists and discovered that the walls of that room extended past the Ottoman Turk floor level, the early Muslim floor level, the Crusader floor level, passing the Byzantine era, and attached to the Roman floor of the late first century. The archaeologists further discovered that the room was, in fact, a synagogue. But it was no ordinary synagogue, which would have had its prayer direction facing toward the temple in plain sight. There were broken plaster portions of the first century wall—with inscribed prayers to Jesus! This was evidently the synagogue church of early Jewish believers in Jesus who in 73 AD returned from Pella in Jordan where they had fled when the Roman general Titus destroyed the Jerusalem temple in 70 AD. This, then, was the "Mother of All Churches," Holy Zion and the Church of the Apostles, and that is why this little room was so important to later Christian art.

And now to the point of our parable. If not to Jerusalem's temple, then, to which Golgotha does the little room's prayer direction face? To the Holy Sepulchre, or to Gordon's Calvary?

Neither. It faces almost exactly between them!

Likewise, there is abundant evidence that KAL 007 landed within a quarter of a mile either to the west of Moneron or a quarter mile to the east of Moneron—with the preponderance of evidence weighted slightly to the east.

"Within a quarter of a mile." KAL 007 is unlikely to have landed farther than a quarter of a mile away from Moneron, as the purpose of KAL 007's making at least two circles was to seek a suitable place close enough to the island so that greater prospects for survival and rescue would be ensured.[133]

"West of Moneron." It was to the west that the Soviet trawler *Uvarovsk* was first directed to search; only later, after nothing was found but a fuel spill from a ship rather than a plane, was Captain Bilyuk ordered to proceed to the north of Moneron. The command to proceed west might well have been necessitated by the fact that many small boats had, according to Admiral Sidorov, already viewed the plane at that position, or might even have seen it land there. Soviet radar trackings, of course, could have indicated KAL 007's landing location relative to Moneron.

In addition, three hours after the shoot-down, the Japanese Maritime Safety Agency (JMSA) had reported that the Japanese Defense Agency (JDA) had tracked an aircraft "100 NM [nautical miles] northeast of Wakkanai, moving in a southwesterly direction." Japan dispatched two patrol vessels and two aircraft and later eight more patrol vessels to a position west of Moneron Island. But Japan's request to enter U.S.S.R. territorial water was denied.[134]

---

[133] See Appendix B

[134] ICAO Report 1983, p. 33

"East of Moneron." Though Soviet and Japanese vessels began to retrieve waterborne debris within three and a half hours of the shootdown, it was nine days later that KAL 007's debris began to appear on the beaches of Wakkanai, on Japan's northernmost island of Hokkaido, and on Sakhalin Island's Port of Nevelsk. But how could debris from KAL 007's "wreckage" float south to the beaches of Hokkaido? If an exploded KAL 007 (whether destroyed in the air by a Soviet missile, or in the water, as we contend, after passengers had been evacuated) had appeared in the waters either to the west of Moneron or to the north of Moneron, the debris would have been borne northward rather than southward. This is because the Tzushima Shio, a brisk (two knots), warm current originating at the Tzushima Straits between Korea and Japan and passing along the coast of Japan and then the coast of Sakhalin and Moneron, is a northerly-flowing current.[135] The only exception to the south-to-north flow in the eastern Tatar Straits is east of Moneron Island, between Moneron and Sakhalin islands, where there are occasional and rather slow (one knot and less) southerly currents. If KAL 007 had been exploded east of Moneron, its wreckage could have floated the approximately 35 miles south to the southern tip of Sakhalin Island, where it would have caught the eastward branch of the Tzushima Shio flowing at a strong 5 to 7 knots into the La Perouse (Soya) Strait separating the Soviet Sakhalin and the Japanese Hokkaido islands—and then, onto the beaches of Wakkanai—40 miles distant from the southern tip of Sakhalin.

With all this in view, a Soviet Naval Specialist's remarks cited in the Izvestiya series are relevant to the issue of locating KAL 007's landing site.

"When we learned that the aircraft had been attacked and that weapons had been used, we began to analyze when it might possibly come down. Ships were ordered to the anticipated area.[136] Several

---

[135] The Tatar Straits does have a south flowing current—the cold Liman current, but this is on the opposite side of the Straits and therefore irrelevant to the issue of KAL 007's landing location.

[136] This is clear evidence that Soviet vessels were ordered to the "crash" site even prior to the "crash." This is relevant to the issue of survivors.

ships headed there at once at full speed. One of them soon reported[137]—
this was two or three hours after the report that the aircraft had been
shot down—that a multitude of small objects could be seen in the
water, presumably, parts of the fragmented Boeing. But the current in
these parts is rapid. And floating objects are constantly borne *south*
[author's emphasis]."[138]

It was also between Moneron and Sakhalin Island that Shifrin's
eyewitness-based information located the Soviet disembarking of passengers and crew from the floating jumbo jet.

Whether, then, east or west of Moneron, it is clear that despite
the USSR's official denials, the exact spot where KAL 007 had landed
soon became the locale of intensive interest and activity. At his Sept.
9, 1983 press conference, Marshal of the Soviet Union and Chief of
General Staff Ogarkov stated that

"We could not give the precise answer about the spot where it
[*KAL 007*] fell because we ourselves did not know the spot in the first
place. And as for assertions in the Western Press that the U.S.S.R. is
hindering searches by the US, Japanese, or any other forces, that does
not correspond to reality at all . . ."

But the General was lying on two counts:

- The Russians had indeed hindered the United States and
  other forces from searching for KAL 007.[139]

- The Russians knew the exact spot within "two and a half
  by four miles" (the size of Moneron Island) where KAL
  007 was to be found. "Ships had been ordered to the
  anticipated area . . ."

That is, it was known with some certainty where KAL 007 would
land—in view of the Soviet High Command radar trackings of KAL
007's flight trajectory after it had been rocketed. And there is no
reason to doubt the success of either the Search and Rescue Mission

---

[137] Possibly the *Uvarovsk.*

[138] As quoted in "Worldwide Issues," 14 February, 1991.

[139] See Appendix C.

involving "rescue helicopters," Border Guards (patrol boats), and the KGB ordered by the Lt. Col. Novoseletski, the Acting Chief of Staff of Smirnykh Air Force Base, at 06:47, just 21 minutes after KAL 007 had been rocketed, or the Search and Rescue Mission involving the Border Guard patrol boats and civilian ships off Moneron Island ordered by Gen. Strogov, the Deputy Commander of the Far East Military District, at 06:54, just 28 minutes after KAL 007 had been rocketed.

Furthermore, Admiral Sidorov stated that within 27 minutes small boats (presumably Border Guard patrol boats and Soviet trawlers) had reached the area of the stricken aircraft.

Within one-half hour of the shoot-down, then, there is evidence that KAL 007 would have been surrounded by a variety of small boats, and KGB General of the Coast Guard Romanenko's boarding party would have gained access to the aircraft and have already boarded it.

The Romanenko Involvement

As KGB General of the Coast Guard assigned to guarding and monitoring the waters between the Soviet Gavan mainland on the west and Sakhalin Island (including Moneron) on the east, General Romanenko was well known to the Japanese Maritime Safety Agency and to the captains of the Japanese trawlers, due to his frequent dealings with incidents involving Japanese fishing infringements in Soviet territorial waters. There are indications that shortly after the KAL 007 incident, things went ill for Romanenko, though there are conflicting reports as to what extent. The CIA report relaying information provided by recent Soviet émigrés states that Romanenko "was reportedly disciplined by Ogarkov, relieved, and sent to the Gulag himself."[140]

Shifrin's informant information indicates that General Romanenko's name no longer appears in the KGB computer system. There are no indications that he had been relieved of his position, retired, or had died. It is as if he had never existed!

---

[140] CIA Report, p. 75.

Hans Ephraimson-Abt, former President of the American Association for Families of KAL 007 Victims and whose daughter Alice was aboard the plane, reports that he had been on official Association business at the Soviet Embassy in East Berlin—business unrelated to the matter of Gen. Romanenko—when he was approached and informed that the man about whom he was seeking information (he was not!), Gen. Romanenko, had committed suicide.[141] In the Soviet Union, of course, state executions were often termed "suicides."

Whatever happened to the General, it is clear that the Soviet authorities considered his conduct in the case of KAL 007 questionable, at best. The CIA Report concluded that, "he had made mistakes and knew too much." The part that Romanenko had played in this tragedy and the probable cause of his being disciplined, banished, and possibly executed, are suggested in the CIA Report in the section entitled "New Evidence From Recent Russian Émigrés."

> "The recent émigrés provide new information that KAL 007 actually ditched successfully in Soviet territorial waters between Moneron Island and Sakhalin Island, and reportedly that many passengers, including Congressman Larry McDonald may have survived. The ditched plane was reportedly recovered intact by KGB Border Guard boats under the command of KGB General Romanenko, and it was stripped of all its surviving passengers and their luggage. The émigrés also report that a Soviet helicopter pilot saw KAL 007 in one piece on the surface of the ocean. It was then towed to Soviet territorial waters near Moneron, and deliberately sunk in shallow waters inside Soviet territorial limits . . . but Gen. Romanenko reportedly did not know what to do with the survivors and their luggages and he forgot to retrieve the black boxes . . ."[142]

Shifrin's information, based on the signed testimony of two Soviet fishermen, indicates that the passengers and luggage were removed from

---

[141] As related by Hans Ephraimson-Abt to the present author.

[142] CIA Report, pp. 74, 75.

KAL 007 and transported aboard patrol boats to Soviet Gavan on the Russian mainland across from Sakhalin Island. Gen. Romanenko was responsible for that action. Further reports indicate that Larry McDonald and the pilot and copilot were separated from the rest of the survivors, again by Romanenko's order, and transported first to Lubyanka Central KGB Prison, and then to Lefortovo Prison.

The Black Boxes

It is not clear whether the Black Boxes were removed while the aircraft was still afloat, or whether, due to Romanenko's oversight, they were left in the plane, only to be retrieved by divers after it had been sunk—by order of Gen. Varennikov, the Deputy Chief of Staff of the Intelligence Directorate of the General Staff.[143]

Gen. Varennikov, arriving on Sakhalin Island on September 1, was to head the first of at least four military inquests concerning the Soviet defense flap over Kamchatka, and to a lesser extent, over Sakhalin, as well as cover-ups proper. These four were:

- The State Commission of the GRU (Intelligence Directorate of the General Staff—headed by Deputy Chief of Staff Gen. Varennikov, under Ogarkov) This commission concerned itself with "damage control" and cover-up, as well as with the matters of inquiry.

- The Commission from the Far East Theater of Operations, headed by Chief of Air Forces Soviet Air Defense Marshal Petr Semenovich Kirsanov (Kirsanov was the first Soviet official to announce—on January 1, 1991—that the Russians had found the wreckage of the plane.)

---

[143] General Varennikov, as well as Marshal Ogarkov and several others, would later be arrested in connection with the October 1991 coup attempt against Gorbachev, but would soon after be released. Their release might indicate the relative strength that they and their supporters still retain, and this may explain the present strength of the continuing Russian cover-up of KAL 007.

- The Commission from the Main Staff of the Soviet Air Defense Forces.

- The Far East Military District Commission.

Prior to Boris Yeltsin's disclosure that the Soviets had, in fact, recovered the Black Box, Shifrin had already provided the exact locations in Russia where the components of the Black Boxes were disassembled and analyzed, with complete details of the personnel involved. The CIA confirmed, in the main, the details of the Shifrin's research. The principal personnel and institution involved were, according to Shifrin's analysis published on July 11, 1991:

"Major-Gen. Subbotin (Military Aviation), technical scientist; Commander of NII ERAT (Scientific Research Institute of Exploitation and Maintenance of the Aviation Equipment) in the town of Lyubertsy, Moscow District; an experienced specialist for investigating air-accidents; took an immediate part in the investigation as a member of the commission . . . personally supervised all the works on deciphering the data from the 'black boxes' brought to his Institute from Sakhalin . . . His present laboratory address is 6, Geogiu Dezh Street, Moscow.

"Col. Tarasenko, Yuvenalii Yuvenalievich, head of department of flight recorders in NRII ERAT in Lyubertsy where the 'black boxes' from KAL 007 were delivered and investigated. In his department, and with his participation, the special rubber container system was created to transport the 'black boxes' with the surrounding water from Sakhalin. Personally headed the work on deciphering the 'black box' data (under Gen. Subbotin's general supervision).

"Antipov, Mikhail Alexandrovich, head of department of objective control systems—'black boxes' at the Moscow machine building plant named after S.V. Ilyushin . . . was the only civilian member of the investigation commission and was sent to Sakhalin to consult and supervise the removal of the 'black boxes' from the plane as the leading Soviet specialist on the American objective control systems."

The CIA study of 1991 confirms the above information in summary: "The black boxes were placed inside special containers of sea water for their shipment to Moscow, in order to preserve their environment. These institutes were at Lyubertsy and the Ilyushin Aircraft Design Bureau both near Moscow.

U.S. Intelligence can confirm that such institutes are located near Moscow and would be logical places for the Soviets to send the black boxes. The identities of the people in Moscow who analyzed the black boxes were: Mikhail Alexandrovich Antipov, Mikhail Yakolovich Shalito[144], Colonel Uvanely Tarasenko, and General Alexandr Subbotin."[145]

The Final Disposition

The removal of the black boxes, as well as the electronic controls, and the evacuation of passengers and crew with their luggage could well have commenced within KAL 007's first half hour on the water. The cargo bay doors, being below water level, could not have been used and the luggage would have been brought up to the main passenger deck and exits through the cargo-to-deck connecting stairs and lift.

There is no reason to doubt that within one hour of KAL 007's landing, passengers and luggage had started an early morning journey westward aboard General Romanenko's flotilla of coast guard ships, passing from the relatively warm waters surrounding Moneron Island through the refrigerated Siberian waters of the southerly-flowing Liman Current, until all were disgorged on the Russian mainland at Soviet Gavan.

---

[144] The fact that the CIA report includes the name of Mikhail Yakolovich Shalito as one of the Soviet experts who analyzed the black boxes whereas Shifrin makes no mention of him indicates that the CIA has knowledge from sources independent of Shifrin.

[145] CIA Report, p. 77.

Within the first hour, or possibly beginning the second hour, the Soviets attached a tow to the aircraft and began a journey which, two or three hours later, would place KAL 007 in its watery grave. The Shifrin and CIA reports differ as to the details but agree in the main. Whereas Shifrin's informants have stated that a Soviet fixed-wing aircraft photographed KAL 007 from above as it was being towed, the CIA Report states that it was a helicopter that photographed the final journey. But, of course, there may well have been multiple photographing by various Soviet aircraft in the process of towing KAL 007. The underwater explosion that was intended to simulate the appearance of a rocket-destroyed aircraft probably occurred east of Moneron, as it is only east of Moneron that there is a north-to-south current—explaining the fact that some of KAL 007's debris were found nine days later south of Sakhalin Island on the northern shore of Hokkaido.

There is yet another incontrovertible piece of evidence that at least some of KAL 007's passengers were rescued. Perhaps, this chapter can best be concluded by citing it. According to the CIA Report, this evidence comes from "sensitive special intelligence." From the nature of the information (electronic intercepts), we may conclude that the special intelligence had come from the National Security Agency, and it is this type of evidence that needs to be publicized and disseminated in a wider way. About four hours after the shoot-down, Soviet Air Defense command posts reported that Soviet pilots were saying that a civilian passenger plane had been shot down instead of a U.S. RC-135 reconnaissance plane, and they (the command posts) were expressing regret, both that they had not downed the RC-135 and that now the Americans would accuse them of killing Americans.

The CIA Report asks how, while flying overhead, could Soviet pilots conclude that Americans were among the passengers? They might conclude from seeing the aircraft's distinctive hump as the plane floated on the water that it was a passenger plane that was shot down, as in 1983 there were no military versions of the Boeing 747. And they might have seen the distinctive bird emblem on the tail of the aircraft—the symbol in use then by Korean Air Lines[146]—but this would not indicate the nationalities of the passengers. The Report would conclude that the only way Soviet pilots could know that Americans had been killed is if they had heard that information on their radios during the time the rescue was actually taking place.

> "Thus the only way that Soviet pilots could possibly have identified the nationality of some of the KAL 007 passengers as Americans, from the air, would have been from possible emergency radio communications which U. S. Intelligence did not intercept, from either the stricken airliner ditched at sea, or from its life rafts, or from Soviet rescue boats."[147]

And so, approximately three and a half hours after KAL 007 had been shot down, the Soviet trawler Uvarovsk, under the command of Captain Ivan Bilyuk, cut into the surfacing debris of the airliner, destroyed underwater just minutes earlier, successfully sealing and darkening Russia's window of opportunity from the occasional and altogether too infrequent troubled, questioning eyes of the West—for these many long years.

---

[146] After the KAL 007 incident, Korean Air Lines would officially change its name to Korean Air, drop flight "007" and would adopt the Yin Yang symbol instead of the bird as its official emblem.

[147] CIA Report, p. 57. A second and prior electronic intercept pertinent to KAL 007 being located may be cited here. According to the CIA Report, page 54, approximately 15 minutes after KAL 007 was rocketed—that is, at 06:41—one of Pilot Osipovich's wingmen reported that he was making "reference point circles," presumably over and around the downed aircraft so that air defense radars could precisely locate it. [According to the Russian ground-to-ground communications appended to the ICAO 1993 Report and "Transcript of Monitored U.S.S.R. Interceptor's Transmissions," Appendix D, Osipovich's three wingmen, two of them flying Sukhoi 15 (call signs 121 and 731) and one flying a MiG 23 (call sign 163) were unable, at least until 06:46:09 (the time of the last recorded transmission), to locate the downed aircraft from the air. Thus, transmissions concerning Americans being killed must have been broadcast after 06:46:09.]

EPILOGUE

Seventeen years have elapsed since the KAL 007 incident, and with the passing of time the memory of events has faded. Overtaken by more recent and broader global configurations, our outrage dissipates, and we forget what previously had provoked us to high moral indignation. Private anguish also diminishes, pushed into the recesses of our consciousness by the vitality of our present relationships with our children, our grandchildren, and our new friends. The pain diminishes, but it does not entirely disappear. The non-disappearance has the power to disrupt the placidity of our present by stark existential confrontations with ourselves.

The American husband of a Korean victim of KAL 007 brought his new wife to Israel in order to examine the claims for passenger survival. Could his first wife have survived? And was she alive now? He left evidently unconvinced, his heart doubtless in a turmoil of conflicting emotions. What if he had been convinced that his first wife had survived? How would that have affected his present marriage? Many of the other surviving spouses had remarried as well. This is the nature of all life-depriving catastrophes.

Life for the Soviet participants of the KAL 007 incident went on as usual, exhibiting what could be considered the normal vicissitudes of Soviet military and political status and career.

Air Force Marshall Petr Semenovich Kirsanov was demoted for his responsibility in the Soviet defense flap over Kamchatka. KGB General Romanenko was demoted, exiled, or executed—most probably for his oversights related to passenger and black box disposition.

Marshall Valentin I. Varennikov, who had arrived at Sakhalin Island within 24 hours of the shoot down in order to head the Secret State Commission and its cover-up, rose to become Deputy Defense

Minister and Commander in Chief of the Ground Forces before his imprisonment (and subsequent release) for the part he played in the October 1991 coup attempt against Gorbachev.

General Ivan Moiseevich Tretyak and General Vladimir L. Govrov were both promoted to the Ministry of Defense in Moscow—the former as Deputy Minister of Defense and Commander in Chief of Soviet Air Defense Forces (1991) and the latter as Deputy Minister of Defense for Civil Defense.

Valery Vladimirovich Ryzhkov, on-duty commander of Radio-Technical Battalion 1845, which had tracked KAL 007's flight, and who was so bitter about his being passed over for promotion, was finally granted that promotion and made commander of the command post of Radio-Technical Battalion 2213 in Mariinskoe Settlement on Soviet Gavan.

But the big winner in the long run (that is, the one who made the biggest jump) was General Anatoli Kornukov, commander of Sokol Air Force Base—the base from which Colonel Gennadie Osipovich's Sukhoi 15 took off in its fateful mission. As told in the words of the International Herald Tribune, January 24-25, 1998 edition:

> "Russian Who Doomed 007
> New Air Chief Ordered '83 Downing of KAL Flight
> Associated Press
> MOSCOW — The Russian Air Force acknowledged Friday that its new chief was the commander who ordered a pilot to shoot down a South Korean jet liner off Sakhalin Island in 1983, killing all 269 people aboard . . ."[148]

General Kornukov, who had retained his position when in 1976 a pilot under his command had defected to Japan with his MiG 25[149]— the most advanced Soviet fighter of the time—also survived the KAL 007 incident, eventually attaining the highest appointment possible in

---

[148] Associated Press. *International Herald Tribune*, Saturday-Sunday, January 24-25, 1998

[149] Lt. Victor Belenko

his field of service—commander of the entire Russian Air Force. Of the many international newspapers which recorded Kornukov's new position, few, if any, noted the fact, so clearly evident in the Russian communiqués appended to the 1993 ICAO report, that Kornukov was but the low general on the totem pole, while those above him who had given Kornukov the order for the shoot down, some, by abdication to his will, were all, apparently, exonerated.[150] These were, in ascending order of their ranks at the time, General Kamenski—Commander of the Far East Military District Air Force, General Strogov—Deputy Commander of the Far East Military District, General Ivan Moiseevich Tretyak—Commander of the Far East Military District, and General Vladimir L. Govrov—Commander of the Far East Theater of Operations.

In the United States, by the mid 1990's, the steam had gone out of Jesse Helms' committee on KAL 007 and its work ceased. This may have been connected to the dismissal of committee Minority Staff Leader Jim Lucier and others active in pushing forward with the investigation.

By 1996, the State Department's official position in the matter of KAL 007's survival was quite clear—and quite official. To the many inquiries forwarded to the State Department by various senators to whom this author had given information relating to passenger rescue, State Department Assistant Secretary for Legislative Affairs, Wendy Sherman, gave the same response:

> "In its final investigative report, ICAO concluded that KAL 007 was hit by at least one of two air-to-air missiles fired from a U.S.S.R. SU-15 interceptor aircraft. There was substantial damage to the aircraft which affected its controllability and the plane was destroyed upon impact with the sea. The wreckage of KAL 007 was located at 46° 33' 32" N—141°19' 41" E, 17 nautical miles north of Moneron Island in interna-

---

[150] The totem pole, most probably, extended through the political echelon up to Yuri Andropov, the Soviet Premier, but that has not, at this time, been verified.

tional waters at about 174 m. depth—over an area of about 60 x 160 m. The report concluded that there were no survivors. The U.S. government accepted the findings of the ICAO report, and believes that no credible evidence has been produced by anyone that contradicts or undermines its conclusions."[151]

"Undermines" is an interesting word in this connection. It implies that the very foundation, upon which a cohesive and stable structure has been erected, is itself being eaten or eroded away—or toppled. And indeed that sort of demolition is what a careful scrutiny would discern. Immediately after the shoot-down, the State Department apparently changed its position concerning Soviet claims to southern Sakhalin Island. This change is implied by State's Geographer's Office issuing a new official map of Sakhalin just three days after the shoot-down. This map had the boundary line dividing Sakhalin Island into north and south removed. The boundary line on State's old official map expressed the United States' recognition of the area north of the boundary line as sovereign Soviet territory, while south of the boundary was recognized as de-facto Soviet occupied, but Japanese-claimed territory. The United States had viewed the final disposition of the southern portion of Sakhalin Island to be decided by the signatory states to the Treaty of San Francisco.[152] In 1947, the United States had even sent a note to the Soviet Union rejecting the Soviet claims to southern Sakhalin.

Does not the elimination of the boundary line on the State Department's official map just three days after the shoot down imply a U. S.-Soviet deal, and could not the collusion expressed by this deal be a pervading factor influencing the conclusions of the United Nations' ICAO report? And would not our acknowledgement of this collusion "undermine" the very processes that led to ICAO's conclu-

---

[151] See Appendix F for full text (example letter to Senator Bob Graham) of State Department letters.

[152] The signatories to the Treaty of San Francisco were to make their determination in accordance with the provisions of the Treaty of Portsmouth—provisions concerned with assigning areas to Japan's sovereignty.

sions and that led ultimately to the final United States position on this matter?

What, then, of the passengers and crew? What about their disposition? Not as much as desired can be said about this matter—yet much more than is commonly imagined.

First, there are the anecdotes—difficult to assess, impossible to dismiss. Walter O'Reilly, President of Forget Me Not, the umbrella organization for various POW/MIA groups, the organization popularly associated with yellow flower distribution, reports that while on official business in the new Russian Federation, he was accosted at the steps of the former Lubyanka Central KGB prison by two men who surreptitiously said to him "We have your congressman." O'Reilly's response was a startled, "No, you don't," as he walked quickly away. He then realized that they must have meant Congressman Larry McDonald. He quickly returned to the steps but the men were gone.

A Christian minister in Long Island, New York, reports that while visiting Russia he had contact with a Russian pastor who claimed that he had been imprisoned for his faith with a group of people whom he believed were the American contingent from KAL 007. They had arrived at the prison the same week as the shootdown. Initially clothed in Western civilian attire, they presently donned the normal prison uniform. This Russian pastor now lives on the west coast of the United States and still has contact with the Christian minister in Long Island, but he refuses to say anything further about the matter, fearing for the safety of his relatives in Russia and for his own safety in the United States. Certain individuals have circulated among the Russian émigrés in his area warning them with threats lest they should ever speak of their prison experiences.

One mother of teenage children—passengers of KAL 007—reports that while on a business trip to China, she received a phone call from one of her children who immediately hung up after telling her not to worry. This mother has no idea how her child located her at her hotel room, but she has no doubts that it was her child.

Another woman, whose husband a computer specialist on board flight 007, received a phone call from an individual whose voice she immediately recognized as her husband's. But the call was abruptly cut off.

And then there is the strange and chilling tale of former Russian academician, David Stavitski, now residing in the United States. In an article published in Aleph, the Russian language US/Israeli publication[143], Stavitski recounts that just three months after the shoot-down of KAL 007, while in the process of preparing for a conference of college teachers in the field of the effects of psychotropic drugs during combat, he had recourse to discussion with a medical colonel named Kodumov. Their discussion led to the use of parapsychology in altering perception. Kodumov informed Stavitski of a program begun at Serbsky Institute near Moscow, which was later adapted at the Sverdlovsk Institute, also near Moscow, for an experimental program called Adnure (parole). Adnure was a program in which captured foreign national subjects were conditioned out of operating from their identities in order to become pliable agents of espionage to be returned to their home countries, responding in all ways as, for example, Americans, but faithful and obedient suppliers to their Soviet "handlers."[154] Kodumov informed Stavitski that he thought the KAL 007 passengers would be used for the Adnure program. What is startling is not that the KAL 007 passengers had been definitely placed at the Adnure project facility (they had not), but that a medical colonel associated with a scientific institute of the Soviet Union could suggest, as a matter of course, the real possibility of captured foreign nationals—among them the passengers of KAL 007—being found in such a horrendous program.

---

[153] "Will Project Adnure Be This Century's Secret?" David Stavitski, Aleph no. 606, 2-9 November, 1995, pp. 42,43.

[154] Adnure seems to be a type of Soviet espionage training facility commonly known as "charm schools"—but with a parapsychological input. The typical charm school operation is currently being popularized (and fictionalized) through a recent book, The Charm School, by Nelson Demille (New York: Warner Books, 1988).

*   *   *

On February 24, 1995, Shifrin's Research Centre for Prisons, Psyche Prisons, and Forced Labor Concentration Camps of the U.S.S.R. published a memorandum including valuable information about the present whereabouts of the KAL 007 survivors—particularly the whereabouts of Congressman Larry McDonald.[155] The following are relevant excerpts from the memorandum:

> "United States Congressman, Dr. Larry McDonald, was taken by special convoy from Khabarovsk to Moscow and initially kept in the inner KGB prison of Lubyanka in Moscow. He was kept in complete isolation and when taken out of his ward for interrogation, was not called by his name but by 'Prisoner No. 3.' Following a number of questionings by KGB head Kruchkov, he was moved to the KGB prison of Lefortovo in Moscow.
>
> "After several months of interrogation in Lefortovo, he was moved once again, this time to a special secret KGB 'dacha' (summer house) in Sukhanova near Moscow, where he continued to be interrogated . . . In approximately 1986—1987, Larry McDonald was transferred to a small local prison near the town of Temir-Tau (Kazakhstan).
>
> "The attempts to locate the present whereabouts of Larry McDonald made by our people in 1993 yielded some results: through talking with the prison wardens of the prison located to the north of Temir-Tau, we learned that sometime in 1987, a prisoner looking like the one in the computer-aged picture of Larry McDonald[156] which was shown to them was brought to their prison from Karaganda by a special transport and was kept on the second floor of the prison building in strict isola-

---

[155] On February 6, 1997, the published results of Centre investigations were conveyed to, among others, United States Congressman Robert K. Dornan (R-California, 46th District) while he was in Israel in connection with Israeli and Palestinian counterclaims to Hebron.

[156] See computer-aged photo in Appendix G.

tion. Against all the regular rules, a table was put in his room and a spring mattress. A stronger than usual electric bulb was brought to the chamber. The food for that prisoner was delivered daily from a civilian restaurant rather than from the prison kitchen, and both the food and the white bread were given to him without the usual limitations—contrary to all prison norms. It was strictly forbidden for anybody to speak with this prisoner and he himself never tried to speak to anyone. For the obligatory daily walk in the prison yard, he was taken separately from all other prisoners. Once a week, a KGB officer would arrive from Karaganda in order to check up on the prisoner. Even this officer would not speak to the prisoner. He would merely inquire of the guard if the prisoner were well, if there had been any special occurrences connected with the prisoner, if anybody had tried to violate the special rules of his confinement.

"In 1990, sometime during the summer, the prisoner was taken by a special convoy in a prison van to the Karaganda transportation prison. Nobody knew then, nor knows now, who this special prisoner was; the envelope containing his file was sealed by the KGB and the prison administration could not open it. The only thing known to them was that the prisoner was to be kept there according to the instructions of the Moscow KGB. Thus far, all the attempts to obtain any additional information through the Karaganda prison have produced no results . . ."

Finally, much has been learned about camps—Gulags—that might possibly be prime locations for not only KAL 007 survivors, but also for POW/MIAs from the United States wars from as far back as World War II.[157] For example, Congressman Dornan had been informed by the Research Centre of an area of the Tigre forest in the Amur River vicinity where three large concentration camps currently operate. Though these camps have never been visited by Westerners

---

[157] See <u>Moscow Bound: Policy, Politics, and the POW/MIA Dilemma</u> (Eureka, CA: Veteran Press, 1993).

(or most probably by anyone else not positively disposed and intimately involved with the Soviet Communist prison system), the immensity of these camps can best be appreciated by the fact that, in winter, smoke can be seen ascending from up to 90 chimneys while each barrack has two or three stoves—that is, this region alone has from 30 to 45 separate barracks!

The United States government, may, if it has the will, do something about this situation. A first step might be the use of NASA satellites to photograph high likelihood areas to determine whether certain concentration and forced labor camps (over 2,500 still remain throughout the former Soviet Union) are populated by foreigners or are "home" to Soviet nationals. Camps populated by Soviet nationals exhibit continual and cyclical prisoner releases, which provide for the buildup of prison towns in adjacent areas to the camps.[158] These towns are absent from the foreign prisoner camps as those prisoners are never released.

High-resolution photos from satellites thousands of miles in space are able to distinguish between full-sized and mini-vans, and are even able to pick up their license plate numbers. There are also powerful low altitude satellites that are capable of locating possible prison sites and making positive verification. One example is the "Code 467" satellite, better know as Big Bird. "Built by Lockheed and first launched on June 15, 1971, the satellite is a massive twelve-ton, fifty-five-foot long spy station build around an extraordinary, super high resolution camera capable of distinguishing objects eight inches across from a height of ninety miles."[159] Examples of the incredible capability of satellite imaging for nonconventional purposes (that is, nonmilitary purposes) are cited in the Wall Street Journal—an Arizona farmer was fined $4000 by the Arizona Department of Water Resource for growing cotton without obtaining the required irrigation permit. Arizona state officials detected the irregularity by comparing their records

---

[158] In most cases, the families of Soviet ex-prisoners were required to join them in these prison towns rather than the ex-prisoners being allowed to return to their original homes.

[159] See discussion in The Puzzle Palace, James Bamford, Penguin Books, New York, 1983, pp 259, 260

of water use permits with photos obtained from the French government's SPOT satellites which had photographed 750,000 acres of Arizona farmland.

Georgia state officials, which have used commercial satellite imaging for monitoring timber use and exploitation as well as for forest surveys, are contemplating a suggestion for the use of satellite photos "to look for objects as small as back yard porches, to check if homeowners have their construction permits in order."

At present, it would cost $6,500 for a satellite to photograph 10 square kilometers with about a 6-foot resolution.

Surely such technology could be put to use for the search and rescue of the 269 unfortunate men, women, and children, victims of what may have been the single most dangerous spark in this century's tinderbox, the Cold War.

Whether by prayer, by recourse to the democratic institutions of pen and pressure, by appeal to public official conscience, or national sense of decency, or by all of these together, the place may be found to wedge a fulcrum and move this recalcitrant world of ours.

Exie's father and cousin, Tay and Edith, Todd's and Alicia's mother Becky, Olivia's and Alexander's father and Olga's husband, Jan, Tomas' and Margaret's daughter Mary Jane, the entire Grenfell family including Noelle, and "little Stacy", Kyung Hwa Park's husband Han Tae, Beatrice Hurst's daughter Francis, Harold's and Lenore's daughter Dianne and grandson Sammy, and all the rest, are worth it.

Jessie Helms would later write Boris Yeltsin, "This event had an element of a personal catastrophe for me, since I was on the parallel flight that night on KAL-015, which departed Anchorage, Alaska about fifteen minutes after KAL-007. Both flights stopped in Anchorage for refueling. I shall never forget mingling with the doomed passengers of KAL-007 in the transit lounge, including two sweet young girls who waved goodby to me when they were called to return to their fatal flight." Those two girls were Noelle and Stacy Grenfell. How can we sit and do nothing!

"XIII CONCLUSION:
KAL 007 PROBABLY DITCHED SUCCESSFULLY,
THERE MAY HAVE BEEN SURVIVORS, THE SOVI-
ETS HAVE BEEN LYING MASSIVELY, AND DIPLO-
MATIC EFFORTS NEED TO BE MADE TO RETURN
THE POSSIBLE SURVIVORS."

Page 77
CIA Republican Staff Study Report

APPENDIX A

For Want of a Zero

In the United States, public perception counts for a great deal. Public officials can be unseated and others put in their place. Under fear of this threat, legislators may be moved to convene committees of inquiry and to hold congressional meetings. The best of these public officials will do so not needing to "fall under fear." These are the ones who act out of conviction. It is also true that the impressions that last are our last impressions. The media plays a great part in informing and forming these impressions. But the media, too, have their sources—and predilections. All of this bears on our perception of the KAL 007 incident.

Did KAL 007 cataclysmically and catastrophically explode and crash—precluding the thought of the possibility of survivors and, of course, precluding the acting and pressing for their rescue? Or did KAL 007 successfully ditch?

If passersby in the street were queried today as to the fate of Korean Airlines Flight 007, most of those able to remember the incident at all would probably reply something on the order of, "It exploded, and everyone died." These are our last and lasting impressions. Yet the original public report which the world had received did not say this. In identical words, Secretary of State George Shultz and Acting Permanent Representative of the U. S. to the U. N., Charles Lichtenstein, in separate public forums on the day of the shoot-down stated, "At 18:26, the Soviet pilot reported that he fired a missile and the target was destroyed. At 18:30 hours, the Korean aircraft was reported by radar at an altitude of 5,000 meters. At 18:38 hours, the Korean plane disappeared from the radar screens."

Most people believe that what the Soviet pilot had reported—mainly, that the "target was destroyed"—was, indeed, true. Most people interpret the phrase "disappeared from the radar screens" to mean that either it had exploded or crashed into the sea. In reality, all that it means is that it was no longer being observed as radar could no longer track it on account of the curvature of the earth/distance of radar factor. It was a modest statement of fact, though both men might well have believed, with most everyone else, that all had died.

But they also stated that after four minutes of flight (later adjusted to five minutes) KAL 007 was acquired by radar at 5,000 meters—i.e. 16,400 feet altitude. That week, media uniformly repeated this. For example, Aviation Week and Space Technology in its September 5 issue stated that, "at 1830 GMT (2:30 p.m. EDT) the transport was monitored at 5,000 meters. Eight minutes later the aircraft was no longer registering on radar."

But a descent from 5,000 meters for eight minutes conforms more to the flight path of an aircraft in gradual descent, leading us to the expectation of a possibly successful ditching and to the good hope for passenger survival and rescue. The average rate of descent (decreasing) actually produced by the analysis of the Russian and Japanese radar trackings—the trackings which were the basis of Shultz's and Lichtenstein's comments—supports this view. One would not derive from all this that a catastrophic explosion had occurred, killing all on board.

But just three days after Secretary of State George Shultz's and Representative Charles Lichtenstein's public announcements, a National Security Agency special intelligence report changed the raw data of 5,000 meters to 500 meters, which, for a short but extremely decisive period of time, became the official reference point for government agencies, and therefore for the media as well. A zero had disappeared. Was it a typographical error—an unexplainable and profound carelessness in such a matter of enormous national importance?[160] Or was the zero intentionally deleted? In any case, an impression was created which persisted from that point on—that none could have

---

[160] CIA report, p. 43.

survived such a disaster and that it would be but foolishness to think otherwise. That impression to this day prevails over against an October 19, 1983, National Security Agency reanalysis of the raw special intelligence data relating to KAL 007. This reanalysis confirmed that the original publicly stated figure of 5,000 meters instead of 500 meters was indeed correct. The erroneous impression prevails even over a June 1991 additional National Security Agency reanalysis of the original September 1, 1983, raw intelligence data as well as an analysis of its subsequent error of September 3, 1983, changing 5,000 meters to 500 meters, and analysis of the October 19, 1983, correction of that error changing 500 meters back to 5,000 meters.[161]

The damage, though, was done. This book is written, in part, to undo that damage and to leave another "lasting impression," leading to a renewed and strengthened resolve to save the innocent victims still alive somewhere within the borders of the former Soviet Union.

[161] CIA report, p. 44.

APPENDIX B

Soviet Deception of
KAL 007's "Crash" Site

The Soviet Pacific fleet, commanded by Admiral Vladimir Vasilyevich Sidorov, set up main salvage operations north of Moneron Island, approximately at coordinates 46°33'32" N-141°19'41" E. The Soviets maintained that that was the site of both KAL 007's crash and, about a month and a half subsequently, its salvage. In addition, American salvage operations under command of W. T. Piotti, Jr., commander of U.S. Surface Combatant Force, Seventh Fleet, was prevented by the Soviets from working their territorial area.

But the transcripts of the real-time military communiqués released by the Russian Federation to the United Nations in 1992 show that that location could not have been the site of Flight 007's water landing or crash, but merely the salvage sight of Flight 007's wreckage (after it had been towed there). The Russian communiqués are quite clear as to KAL 007's true landing location—within Soviet territorial waters.

Flight 007 had crossed the Kamchatka Peninsula from the North East, traversed the international waters of the Sea of Okhotsk, and entered over Sakhalin Island from Terpinee Bay in Sakhalin' northeast.

Kornukov: (6:24)
Comrade General, Kornukov, good morning, I am reporting the situation. Target 60-65 [*KAL 007*] is over Terpinee Bay tracking

240, 34km from the state border, the fighter from Sokol is 6km away. Locked on . . .

KAL 007 was flying in a south westerly direction and two minutes prior to being struck by a missile had almost traversed Sakhalin Island and was about to fly out into the international waters of Tatar Bay.

Kornukov: (6:24)
Oh [*obscenities*], how long [*does it take him*] to go to attack position, he is already getting out into neutral waters. Engage afterburner immediately. Bring in the MiG 23 as well, . . . while you are wasting time, it will fly right out.

And it is clear that from two minutes after missile strike, beginning at 6:28 a.m., that KAL 007 has survived the attack and is maneuverable. Six minutes after this, at 6:34 is the time of first indication that the Russians knew KAL 007's exact location—spiraling down once again in Soviet territory over Moneron Island.

Lt. Col. Gerasimenko: (6:34)
Turning left, right, apparently it is descending.

Gen. Kornukov: (6:36)
It is over Moneron.

Flight Controller Titovnin: (6:38)
Descending . . . and lost over Moneron.

KAL 007 had, thus, once again entered Soviet territorial waters.

Lt. Col. Novoseletski: (6:38)
So, the task. They say it has violated the State border again now?

Flight Controller Titovnin:
Well, it is the area of Moneron, of course, over our territory.

Lt. Col. Novoseletski:
Get it! Get it! Go ahead, bring in the MiG 23.

It is clear that the Russian military commanders considered Soviet territorial Moneron Island itself, not international waters to the north, to be the site of KAL 007's expected set down. And, it was to Moneron Island itself that Gen. Strogov at 29 minutes after missile strike, directed nearby ships.

Gen. Strogov: (6:55)
What ships do we have near Moneron Island, if they are civilian, send [them] there immediately.

It is evident from the above, that, from the very first moments after the attack, top Soviet military commanders, beginning at the apex with the deputy commander of the Soviet Far East Military District, General Strogov, knew that KAL 007 was alive and well and knew precisely its location—four mile long, two and a half mile wide Moneron Island. We may, therefore, conclude that the Soviet's search and subsequent salvage a month and a half later, mainly in international waters to the north of Moneron Island, was intentionally misleading and an audacious ruse—successful beyond all expectation!

The now declassified United States Surface Combatant Force Seventh Fleet *After Action Report* chart of the Moneron—Sakhalin (see Appendix G) area clearly shows the only possible area that KAL 007 could have flown from Terpinee Bay in the northeast of Sakhalin to Moneron Island in the southwest [present author's insertion of KAL 007's flight path and chart legend].[162]

---

[162] This is the only area that could be overflown by KAL 007 on a flight path from Terpinee Bay to Moneron Island that would also traverse, as required by the Soviet ground-to-ground communication, Soviet territory, then international waters, and once again Soviet territory.

APPENDIX C

Soviet Interference With Joint U.S., Japanese, and South Korean Search & Rescue Operations

The joint search and rescue operations were doomed to failure from the start. Whereas the Soviets deployed dummy searches within Soviet territorial waters north of Moneron Island, the U. S.—led forces were, on the other hand, prevented by Soviet warnings and harassment from entering Soviet waters. Lyman Helms, Federal Aviation Agency Administrator, stated at a hearing of ICAO on Sept. 15, 1983, "The U.S.S.R. has refused to permit search and rescue units from other countries [U.S., Japan, South Korea] to enter Soviet territorial waters to search for the remains of KAL 007. Moreover, the Soviet Union has blocked access to the likely crash site and has refused to cooperate with other interested parties, to ensure prompt recovery of all technical equipment, wreckage, and other material"[163] In addition, an intelligence flap had occurred which prevented "a precise overall search plan at the outset." W. T. Piotti, Jr., commander of the U.S. Surface Combatant Force Seventh Fleet, would report to commander of the Seventh Fleet in the U.S. Search and Salvage After Action Report (now declassified), dated November 15, 1983:

> "All intelligence data ultimately received by the task force commander was available within various U.S. and Japanese agencies by 6 September [six full days after the shoot-down!]. The earliest that the task force received the all source intelli-

[163] Congressional Record, Sept. 20, 1983, pgs S12462—S12464.

gence data in its entirety was 14 October, almost a month and a half after the shoot down. This prolonged flow of information had a direct impact on search planning and effectiveness."

But by far the most serious forms of opposition to the U. S. search for KAL 007 had come from Soviet harassment and threats. These include aerial simulations of low-flying attacks on ships approaching the area of Soviet "search" operations, setting false pingers in (successful) attempts to attract U.S. vessels to incorrect and innocuous locations, actual attempts at ramming and threats to ram, and cutting the moorings of the "allied" vessels. Commandeered and enlisted Soviet vessels were involved in these attacks.[164]

"The large majority of Soviet harassing/embarrassing maneuvers were conducted by naval auxiliaries and fishing vessels."[165]

Commander Piotti would list the following hostile Soviet maneuvers at sea:

> "Maneuvers which prevented ships towing search sensors from making good their programmed search track, maneuvers with significant potential for cutting/fouling the umbilicals of towed sensors or the deep drone and extremely close approaches to moored Japanese charter ships which their masters believed risked collision or damage to their moors (which in several cases did occur). It appeared at the time, and remains so in retrospect, that the Soviets deliberately harassed and sought to intimidate the Masters of the Japanese chartered ships."[166]

---

[164] The Republican Saff/CIA Study considered most of these and other Soviet acts as clear violations of the 1972 <u>Incident at Sea Agreement</u> between the U.S. and the Soviet Union. In particular, it lists the following: "Attempted ramming of U.S. and allied ships, presenting false flag and false light signals, locking on the radar guidance of their weapons against U.S. ships, and even sending an armed boarding part to threaten to board a Japanese Auxiliary vessel chartered by the U.S. Navy search task force." P. 64

[165] After Action Report, p. 14.

[166] ibid., p. 12.

One subject of repeated harassment and even attempted ramming was the Japanese ship *Maru NR3*.

> "Soviet ship maneuvers frequently continued to hamper search operations. On several occasions, this caused delay of mission accomplishment. Close escort, including interposition in risk of collision situations, was not sufficient to prevent the intimidation of the first Master of *Maru NR3*, who twice slipped his moor, rather than remain in what he considered a vulnerable position."[167]

For a fascinating corroboration of the Soviet harassment on this particular vessel as well as corroborating of Commander Piotti's assertion that the Soviets employed false pingers to divert and confuse the allied endeavors, we may turn to a Soviet seaman's report published in the *Izvestiya* series and quoted in "World Wide Issues," 31 May 1991:

> "I recall: there was a moment when Japanese search vessel *Keiko-Maru No. 3* (or *Kaiko-Maru No. 3*) dropped anchor next to *Mirchink*; this vessel had a self-propelled underwater search apparatus, controlled from the vessel via cable. The operational radius of the apparatus from the mother vessel is, if I am not mistaken, two to 2.5 kilometers . . . At that time the TOF commander, Admiral Sidorov, gave an order—immediately equip a trawler stationed on Sakhalin with grapnels (devices to cut mine mooring cables or hawsers) and send it to a station next to the *Keiko-Maru*. As soon as the vessel lowered its apparatus, the trawler was supposed to cut the control cable of the Japanese . . . See how far it went: this was outright banditry! The only thing that saved the *Keiko-Maru* was the false "pinger" planted by our Navy. The Japanese also took the bait of its beacon signal and went to the wrong area."

---

[167] ibid., p. 13.

And so the Soviets not only safely absconded with KAL 007's surviving passengers, they also successfully kept U.S.-led forces at bay, preventing them from seeing and understanding that the "wreck" that their lead salvage vessel, the *Mikhail Mirchink*, was bringing up—was nothing but a ruse.

APPENDIX D

How The Plane Was Lost

Delayed one hour because of strong tail winds,[168] KAL 007 departed Anchorage International Airport at 13:00 GMT (4:00 a.m. Alaskan time). Climbing, the jumbo jet turned left, seeking its assigned route J501, which would soon take it onto the northernmost of five 50-mile wide passenger plane air corridors that bridge the Alaskan and Japanese coasts. These five corridors are called the NOPAC (North Pacific) routes. KAL 007's particular corridor, Romeo 20, passed just 17 1/2 miles from Soviet airspace off the Kamchatka coast. Though the Boeing 747 was capable of being navigated by Long Range Navigation (LORAN)[169]—a less up-to-date system relying on navigational guidance aids external to the aircraft—its principal method of navigation was the Inertial Navigation System (INS).

The INS consisted of three independent, self-contained, but electronically linked units guiding the aircraft according to nine "waypoint" coordinates, some of which were "punched" into the units prior to flight. If more than nine were required, number 10 (and subsequent) coordinates were entered during the flight, replacing waypoint entries overflown and vacated. Korean Airlines received its computerized flight plan from an independent supplier company, Continental Air Service. This plan would designate the following nine waypoints for KAL 007's route from Anchorage, Alaska, to Seoul, South Ko-

---

[168] It was the practice of Korean Airlines to sometimes delay a flight so that it would not arrive at Kimpo Airport in Seoul, Korea prior to 6:00 a.m., as customs and passenger handling personnel began their operations at that time.

[169] LORAN uses a "master" land station and two "slave" stations that transmit low or medium frequency signals. The intersection of transmission lines of pairs of such stations establishes a plane's location.

rea—BET (Bethel), NABIE, NEEVA, NIPPI, NOKKA, NOHO, IFH (Inkfish), MXT (Matsushima), and GTC (Niigata). Each INS unit (two of which were actually used for navigation, the third being a reserve) utilized gyroscopes and accelerometers[170] which minutely and continuously (seven times per second) adjusted (through the automatic pilot) the aircraft in flight in conformity with these coordinates, taking into account changing wind, velocity, weight, and other conditions.

Each unit is comprised of three sub-units:

1. ´ An Inertial Navigation Unit which senses both the horizon and the various movements of the aircraft as it performs the necessary computations to guide the plane along its desired track. The INU is housed in the electronics bay of the aircraft.

2. A Control Display Unit, containing digital readout windows for navigational data as well as pilot data entry options. The CDU is located in the flight deck.

3. A Mode Selection Unit, used for navigational mode engagement. The MSU is located on the flight deck.

Ironically, the same space-age technology that produced the INS's ability to navigate without reference to external aids made it possible for the Soviet salvage ship *Mikhail Mirchink* to stabilize itself dynamically over KAL 007's wreckage, minutely compensating for wind and water changes.

KAL 007 never reached its assigned transoceanic route Romeo 20. Seven to ten minutes after takeoff, the jumbo jet began to deviate[171] to the right of its prescribed flight path—a deviation which would gradually increase until, approximately three and a half hours after takeoff, it would enter Russian territory just north of Petropavslovsk

---

[170] The accelerometers detect changes in the aircraft's motion (any direction) in reference to the gyroscopic lines.

[171] ICAO 1983 report, p. 5.

on the Kamchatka Peninsula. Home to the Soviet Far East Fleet Inter Continental Ballistic Missile Nuclear Submarine base, as well as several air fields, Petropavslovsk was bristling with weaponry.

At 28 minutes after takeoff, civilian radar at Kenai, on the eastern shore of Cook Inlet and 53 nautical miles southwest of Anchorage, with a radar coverage of 175 miles west of Anchorage, tracked KAL 007 more than six miles north of where it should have been. Where it should have been was a location "fixed" by the nondirectional radio beacon (NDB) of Cairne Mountain. The NDB navigational aid operates by transmitting a continuous three-letter identification code which is picked up by the airborne receiver, the Automatic Direction Finder (ADF). Cairne Mountain was KAL 007's first assigned navigational aid out of Anchorage Airport. Something was going wrong.

That night, Douglas L. Porter was the controller at Air Route Traffic Control Center at Anchorage, assigned to monitor all flights in that section, recording their observed position in relation to the fix provided by the Cairne Mountain nondirectional beacon. Porter later testified that all had seemed normal to him.[172] Yet he apparently failed to record[173], as required, the position of two flights that night—and only two: KAL 007, carrying Democratic Congressman McDonald and 268 others, and KAL 015, carrying Republican Senators Jesse Helms of North Carolina and Steven Symms of Idaho, Congressman Carroll J. Hubbard Jr. of Kentucky, and others,[174] which followed KAL 007 by several minutes.

KAL 007 continued on its night journey, having previously received clearance (13:02:40 GMT) to proceed "direct Bethel" when able. Bethel is a small fishing village on the western tip of Alaska, 350 nautical miles west of Anchorage. It is the last U. S. mainland navigational point (but not the last land point), and the first of a series of required reporting stations (KAL 007 was to do the reporting) that

---

[172] Testimony of Douglas L. Porter, U.S. District Court for the District of Columbia, October 6, 1984.

[173] KAL 007: the Coverup, Summit Books, New York 1987, Pg. 37

[174] Senators Helms, Symms, and Congressmen McDonald and Hubbard had been invited by the president of South Korea to participate in the celebration of the 30th year commemoration of the U.S.-Korea Mutual Defense Pact.

would guide KAL 007 along its way—a sort of obligatory external "back-up" verification system designed to confirm the accuracy of KAL 007's internally based Inertial Navigational System.[175]

There were two navigational elements operative at Bethel. The first was the VOR (Very High Frequency Omni-Directional Range) navigational radio station. This apparatus emitted Morse code signals (providing its station identity) at regular intervals in all directions (omnidirectional). If KAL 007 had been using Bethel's VOR station as a course provider, the aircraft had only to ride one of these emitted signal radials "home" in order to be brought to destination. The pilot (or copilot, who also had a receiver before him) had only to ensure that the VOR needle remained centered in order to be certain that he was on course. That is, KAL 007 had only to "ride the radial." However, KAL 007 was not to use the VOR Bethel station as a course provider—the Inertial Navigation System would do that—but as a reporting point.

The second navigational apparatus available at Bethel was the DME (Distance Measuring Equipment). "When tuned to a DME equipped ground facility, the airborne DME sends out paired pulses at a specific spacing. This is the *interrogation*. The ground facility receives the pulses and then transmits back to the interrogating aircraft a second pair of pulses with the same spacing but on a different frequency. The airborne DME measures the elapsed time required for the roundtrip signal exchange and translates that time into nautical miles and time to the station as well as the aircraft's current ground speed."[176] But the VOR and the DME operate as one. [177] Having

---

[175] Korean Airlines required use of the North Pacific Operations Manual, which stipulates that the last land-based navigational aid for oceanic flights (Bethel) be used to verify INS accuracy.

[176] Aeronautical Knowledge, Paul E. Illman, McGraw-Hill, New York, 1995, p. 281.

[177] After Bethel, KAL 007's waypoints were not on its "straight line" flight trajectory (the Great Circle). If KAL 007 had no DME, it would have had to follow radials (like "connect the dots") to its planned destination, rather than following the planned straight line trajectory. With DME, the pilots, once having intercepted the radial, would know the distance to the emitting VOR station, and could calculate the straight line trajectory.

verified by the Morse code that he had the right station, Captain Chun would have dialed in the VOR frequency, and that would have given him both the VOR and the DME. The VOR (and the DME) at Bethel were part of a navigational complex called TACAN for Tactical Air Navigation. Hence, it received the acronym VORTAC.

Bethel's Korean Airline procedure required Flight 007 to verify its position through VOR/DME. Apparently, it did not do so, for at 50 minutes after takeoff, military radar at King Salmon, Alaska, tracked KAL 007 at a full 12.6 nautical miles north of where it should have been.

In addition, the Horizontal Situation Indicator's needle would have alerted the pilots of their course deviation. This is because the cockpit HSI console needle, capable of showing deviation only up to eight miles, would be "pegged" all the way to the side. The pilots, thus, should have known that they were at least eight miles off course![178] Despite this, strangely enough, at 13:49, the pilots were reporting that they were on course! "007, Bethel at forty niner." And so, fifty minutes after takeoff, military radar at King Salmon, Alaska acquired KAL 007 at more than 12.6 miles off course. It had exceeded its permissible leeway of deviation by six times! (Two nautical miles an hour error is the permissible drift from course set by INS.)

---

[178] An aircraft HSI generally has an image of a plane directly above the Horizontal Situation Indicator's needle when the aircraft is on course. A needle pointing to the left or to the right of the image would indicate that the plane is deviated left or right of the course. KAL 007's HSI needle would have been pegged all the way to the right (North). ICAO expanded on the Horizontal Situation Indicator's capability of showing course deviation. The pilots could have known that they were off course by looking at the HSI in front of each of them. Though the HSI was primarily designed to show the aircraft's situation with regard to the horizon, the 747's HSI contained an indicator to register deviation from plotted course. "Indications [of being on course] available to the crew would have been a reducing or zero track bar displacement with the HSI display set to INS and a similar reducing or zero cross track error on the CDUs [consoles]. There would have been a similar effect with the VOR track displacement…"—ICAO report 1993, p. 42, sect. 2.4.4.

Furthermore, pilot and copilot should also have been aware of the aircraft's serious deviation because now, much more than 12 miles off course, KAL 007 was too far from Bethel for the pilots to make their required Very High Frequency (VHF) radio reports, and had to relay these reports via KAL Flight 015, just minutes behind it and on-course (KAL 007 would have to rely on KAL 015 three times to transmit its reports to increasingly out of range way stations). That alone should have alerted them.

At one point in this section of its flight, (14:43 GMT) KAL 007 put a call through a navigational "hookup," the International Flight Service Station on High Frequency. Flight 007, now too distant to speak directly with Anchorage Controller through Very High Frequency, was transmitting its message indirectly using High Frequency.[179] The message was a change in the Estimated Time of Arrival (ETA) for the next waypoint called NEEVA—delaying by four minutes the ETA that KAL 015 had previously relayed on behalf of KAL 007. Since a revised ETA could only be calculated by means of readout information presented by KAL 007's Inertial Navigation Systems central display unit, pilot and copilot were once again presented with the opportunity of verifying their position and becoming aware of their enormous deviation.

Halfway between waypoint NABIE and the next required reporting waypoint, NEEVA, KAL 007 passed through the southern portion of the United States Air Force NORAD buffer zone. This zone, monitored intensively by U. S. Intelligence assets, lies north of Romeo 20, KAL 007's designated air route, and is off-limits to civilian aircraft. KAL was apparently undetected—or, if detected, unreported.

And so KAL 007 continued its night journey, ever increasing its deviation—60 nautical miles off course at waypoint NABIE, 100 nautical miles off course at waypoint NUKKS, and 160 nautical miles off course at waypoint NEEVA[180]—until it penetrated Kamchatka's borders.

At 15:51 GMT (two hours and 51 minutes after taking off from

---

[179] At waypoint NABIE, KAL 007 was too far north to make radar contact with the Very High Frequency Air Traffic Control relay station on St. Paul Island. KAL 015 relayed for KAL 007.

[180] ICAO report 1993, p. 45, sect. 2.8.1.

Anchorage, Alaska) according to Soviet sources, KAL 007 "bumped" the Soviet buffer zone of Kamchatka Peninsula.[177] The buffer zone was generally considered to extend 200 km. from Kamchatka's coast and is technically known as a Flight Information Region (FIR). Within that region, aircraft would be queried by Soviet interceptors emitting a signal to the unidentified aircraft. An apparatus called a transponder would squawk back the aircraft's four-digit code, identifying the plane—if it were a Soviet plane. A non-Soviet block plane would not respond, but this in itself registered a negative identification. The pilots of the intruding aircraft would be unaware of the Soviet query. This system is similar to the U. S. military's Identification Friend or Foe (IFF).

The 200 km. buffer zone is counterpart to the United States' Aerospace Defense Identification Zone (ADIZ), but the 100 km. radius of the buffer zone nearest to Soviet territory had the additional designation of Air Defense Zone. Heightened surveillance measures would be taken against any non-Soviet aircraft entering the Air Defense Zone.

August 31/September 1, 1983 was the worst possible night for KAL 007 to "bump the buffer" for a complexity of reasons—all of them ominous. It was but a few short hours before the time that Marshal Ogarkov, Soviet Chief of General Staff, had set for the test firing of the SS-25, an illegal mobile Intercontinental Ballistic Missile (ICBM).[178] The SS-25 was to be launched from Plesetsk, the

---

[181] A U. S. State Department release designates 1551 GMT as the time KAL 007 penetrated the Soviet buffer zone. This time was probably ascertained through U. S. eavesdropping of Soviet radar and voice transmissions by two U. S. Air Force Electronic Security Command Groups—the 6981st located at Elmendorf Air Force Base in Anchorage, Alaska; and the 6920th at Misawa Air Force Base on Honshu Island, Japan.

[182] The SS-25 was in violation of the SALT II agreements on three counts:

1. It was a new kind of ICBM (the first mobile one ever launched).

2. Its telemetry was encoded and encrypted. When a test ICBM reentry vehicle approaches the target, it emits vital data relating to its velocity, trajectory, throw-weight, and accuracy by means of coded (symbolized) and encrypted (scrambled) electronic bursts, which are then

launch site in northwest Russia which was used for test firing of solid fuel propellant ICBMs—24 minutes later to land in the Klyuchi target area on the Kamchatka Peninsula.[183]

Prior to his appointment as Marshal of the Soviet Union and Chief of the General Staff, General Ogarkov had been Chief of the Main Operation Directorate of the General Staff and, as such, had begun and had directed the Strategic Deception Department, or "Maskirovka," which was charged with hiding Salt 2 violations from United States intelligence. On August 31/September 1, Soviet aerial "jammers" under Maskirovka were sent aloft to prevent United States intelligence eyes and ears from obtaining the illegal SS 25's telemetry data.

And indeed, United States intelligence eyes and ears were wide open and unblinking that night—an RC-135 Boeing 707 reconnaissance plane was "lazy eighting" off the Kamchatka peninsula coast electronically "sucking in" emissions.

Exactly which emissions the 707 was collecting depended on which of two versions of the RC-135—code-named "Rivet Joint" and "Cobra Ball," respectively—happened to be deployed that night. Rivet Joint, based at Eielson Air Force Base south of Fairbanks, Alaska, was furnished with cameras, SLAR (side-looking radar) and an array of advanced electronic equipment designed to eavesdrop on in-the-air and on-the-ground conversations, locate and decipher radar signals, "spoofing"[184] (i.e. simulating electronically and otherwise near intrusions of the border thus turning on Soviet radar stations), and tripping and recording the enemy's "order of battle."[185]

---

decoded and decrypted by Soviet on-ground intelligence gathering stations.

3.   The missile as a whole was too large for its reentry vehicle (dummy warhead), raising suspicion that the missile was being developed for new and more advanced warheads than allowable.

[183] Liquid propellant ICBMs were launched from Tyuratam in southwest Russia.

[184] See footnote number 27 on page 26 for the transcript of a Soviet shoot down of a U.S. electronic intelligence aircraft on a "spoofing mission" over Soviet Armenia on Sept. 2, 1958.

[185] Technically, "spoofing involves sending back radar signals multiplied into ghost images.

Cobra Ball, based on Shemya Island on the tip of the Aleutian Island chain, similarly equipped as the Rivet Joint 707 but with much more apparatus, stayed far from the borders of the Kamchatka peninsula waiting for the precise moment of an Intercontinental Ballistic Missiles reentry in order to capture the missile's telemetry signals.[186]

Rivet Joint and Cobra Ball were both under the command of the Air Force's Strategic Air Command (SAC), but the personnel operating the electronic equipment were signal intelligence specialists of the Electronic Security Command (ESC) under the authority of the National Security Agency (NSA). The NSA was charged with the responsibility of gathering and deciphering "raw" intelligence data. This raw data was collected from supersensitive apparatus aboard aerial platforms such as the RC-135, on land collection stations such as that on Wakkanai on the northernmost Japanese Island of Hokkaido (it was from this Wakkanai station that the Japanese radar track of KAL 007's descent had been obtained), and the Misawa Air Base on the main Japanese Island of Honshu. Raw data was even collected from under the sea—from strings of underwater movement and pressure sensors, and from listening devises that are capable not only of "fixing" a ship and its type, but of ascertaining its name, port of departure, destination, and probable mission.

The raw intelligence data then underwent preliminary analysis at various collection platforms and stations, and then, in the far east, were beamed 23 thousand miles up to a geosynchronous satellite (one whose orbit around the world was correlated with the rotation of the earth around its axis in such a way that it remained continually "motionless" over a designated portion of the earth). From this satellite, the raw data was beamed to the NSA facility at Pine Gap, Australia, and from there relayed to NSA headquarters at Fort Meade, Maryland. At Fort Meade, the data was further analyzed and then distributed to various intelligence services of the United States government.

The collection stations and platforms around the world operated

---

[186] The CIA/Republican staff study fixes the RD-135 as Cobra Ball and that the aircraft was already back on its runway on Shemya Island and had been for about an hour when KAL 007 was shot down. Both were in the air (and about 75 miles apart) when KAL 007 entered Kamchatka airspace.

in an on-spot evaluation of the critical nature of the raw material they collected and analyzed. An evaluation of highest priority was called a "Critic Report." A Critic Report had to be at the desks of both the President's National Security Adviser and the Director of the NSA within ten minutes of evaluation at the collection station. In practice, Critic Reports usually reach their destinations within five minutes. It is rare for there to be more than two Critic Reports a year.[187]

Most commentators believe that the KAL 007 incident fully warranted a Critic Report. After all or most of the ramifications became apparent, Senator Helms would write Boris Yeltsin, "One of the greatest tragedies of the Cold War was the shoot-down of the Korean Airlines Flight KAL 007 by the armed forces of what was then the Soviet Union on September 1st, 1983 . . . The KAL 007 tragedy was one of the most tense incidents of the entire Cold War."[188]

It is almost certain, then, that United States intelligence assets, poised that night to receive all that the Soviets emitted, were in position to follow KAL 007's incursion into the Soviet buffer zone off Kamchatka. In fact, they were charged to do so. The RC-135 Rivet Joint would have seen Kamchatka's radar positions "light up" one after another and would have heard the chatter at dozens of command posts. James Bamford, author of The Puzzle Palace and an expert on the operations of the United States National Security Agency explains:

> "The RC-135 is designed for one purpose—it's designed for eavesdropping . . . There's almost no way that the aircraft could not have picked up the indications of Soviet activity: Soviet fighters taking off, Soviet defense stations going into higher states of readiness, higher states of alert."[189]

---

[187] Next in priority were "E-grams," with an outer reception time of 20 minutes. "Spot Reports" came next in priority at 30 minutes, and "Klieg Lights" after that. This whole structure of communications, with numerous other facets of function and operation, are subsumed under the acronym of CRITICOM—Critical Intelligence Communication System.

[188] Senator Helms' letter of December 10, 1991, to Boris Yeltsin. See Appendix F.

[189] As quoted by David Pearson, KAL 007: The Coverup, p. 156.

Most probably Cobra Ball's radar (as well as River Joint's) would have acquired KAL 007 in its flight traversing the RC-135's area of detection. The Soviet Union would contend that not only was there an RC-135 in proximity to KAL 007 as the passenger plane neared the coast of Kamchatka, but that their proximity to each other was premeditated for United States intelligence-gathering purposes.

> "On 31 August, at 17.45 Moscow time (02.45 Kamchatka time on 1 September) an RC-135 reconnaissance aircraft was flying southeast of Karaginski Island. In this area it closed with the aeroplane performing flight KAL 007. Both aircraft were capable of monitoring the situation in the air with their airborne equipment. However, no reaction to the close approach of these aeroplanes to each other took place in the air and they continued to fly on parallel headings for 10 minutes. This confirms that the joint flight of the two aeroplanes was not coincidental, but was planned in advance."[190]

The Soviets would also contend that KAL 007's entire flight—from the time prior to its entry into Soviet airspace off Kamchatka, until it was shot down— "dovetailed" with three passes of a United States Ferret-D intelligence gathering satellite, which would have therefore been apprised of KAL 007's progress into airspace over supersensitive Soviet military installations.

> "Ferret-D appeared over Chukotka at 18.45 Moscow time on 31 August and flew for about 12 minutes east of Kamchatka and in Kurile Islands. On this orbit the satellite was able, immediately prior to the incursion of the intruder aeroplane into Soviet airspace, to zero in on Soviet radio facilities . . . in a routine state of alert and pinpoint their location and level of activity . . .
>
> "On its second orbit Ferret-D appeared . . . at the mo-

---

[190] Preliminary Information on the Progress of the U.S.S.R. Investigation of the accident to a South Korean Aeroplane on 1 September 1983—Appendix F, Restricted, U.S.S.R. Attachment to ICAO report of 1983, p. F11.

ment when the intruder aeroplane penetrated Soviet airspace—
it was over the Kamchatka area. The aeroplane's violation of
the State frontier forced Soviet monitoring facilities to step up
substantially their level of operation. All of this was recorded
by the Ferret-D spy satellite . . .

"Finally, the ensuing orbit of Ferret-D coincided with the
third and last stage of the intruder aeroplane's flight over
Sakhalin. In this interval it was able to record the operation of
all the additional Soviet Air Defense Command electronic
facilities on Sakhalin Island and the Kurile Ridge and in
Primorski Kray."

There were also powerful land and sea radar arrays that could
well have tracked KAL 007 as it approached and entered Soviet territory. These were Cobra Judy aboard the U.S.S. Observation Island,
then off the coast of Kamchatka; Shemya Island's Cobra Dane line of
sight radar with the capability of tracking an airplane at 30 thousand
feet altitude through an area covering 400 miles (the curvature of the
earth being its limiting factor); and Shemya Island's Cobra Talon, an
over the horizon (OTH) "backscatter" radar array with a range from
575 miles to 2,070 miles. Cobra Talon operated by bouncing its emissions off the ionosphere (deflection) to the other side of the line of
sight horizon, thus acquiring its targets. These radar arrays had capability for both surveillance and tracking. Whether this capability was
actualized in the case of Flight 007 is currently unknown. The security "blanket" is a thick one!

We do know that the United States Air Force radar stations at
Cape Newenham and Cape Romanzoff in Alaska not only had the
capability to track all aircraft heading toward the Russian Buffer Zone,
but they were required to do so by Air Force Regulation 60-1.[191]
They were furthermore required to warn the straying aircraft on emergency frequency, and to warn the pertinent Air Traffic Control Cen-

[191] The Cape Newenham and Cape Romanzoff radars monitored at the NORAD
Regional Operations Command Center were but two of twelve comprising
the United States Alaskan Distant Early Warning/Aircraft Control and Warning (DEW/ACW) System.

ters so that they too could attempt to warn the straying aircraft. Well within range of these radar sights, KAL 007 had veered directly toward Kamchatka.

That night KAL 007 plunged into the Russian 200 kilometer buffer zone, then the 100 kilometer Air Defense Zone, and then it was over Russian territory with no one to stop it.

There was one last navigational aid to warn the crew. With consoles at the knees of both pilot and copilot, the plane's weather radar[192] could have alerted them to the fact that they were no longer flying over water, as they ought to have been. Weather radar has two modes—land mapping for clear weather, when it would be possible to look down and see water or land masses as well as the contours of the coast lines and the weather surveillance mode for cloudy weather, when it is necessary to "see through" clouds in order to detect dangerous thunderstorms. In land mapping mode, KAL 007 had only to make sure that the land mass of Kamchatka and the Island string of the Kurile chain would remain to the right. That night, however, KAL 007's weather radar was probably not in land mapping mode, for the weather was inclement. The International Civil Aviation Organization's meteorological analysis would conclude that, "there was extensive coverage of low, medium, and high level clouds over southern Kamchatka associated with an active cold front."[193] ICAO's analysis of KAL 007's weather radar functioning would state, "it was concluded that the radar was not functioning properly or that the ground mapping capability was not used."[194]

Unsuspectingly, KAL 007 crossed the Kamchatka peninsula exiting its airspace at 17:08 GMT[195], and while over the international waters of the Sea of Okhotsk nearing the coast of Sakhalin, a "welcome" was in frantic preparation 33 thousand feet below—documented

---

[192] KAL 007's Bendix radar had a maximum range of 200 NM with a 180° scan capability.

[193] ICAO 1983, section 1.7.1., p. 9.

[194] ICAO 1983, p. 45. Section 2.9.1.

[195] 17:08 GMT was the exact time for both KAL 007's exiting Soviet Airspace over Kamchatka and its estimated time of arrival (ETA) at waypoint Nippi. At Nippi, Flight 007 would no longer be controlled by US airtraffic.

by the transcripts of the Russian military ground-to-ground communications submitted by the Russian Federation and appended to the 1993 ICAO report.

General Kornukov: (6:13)
Chaika

Titovnin:
Yes, sir.
He sees [*it*] on the radar screen, he sees [*it*] on the screen. He has locked on, he is locked on, he is locked on.

Kornukov:
No answer, Roger. Be ready to fire, the target is 45-50 km from the State border.
Officer in charge at the command post, please, for report.

Titovnin:
Hello.

Kornukov:
Kornukov, please put Kamenski on the line. Kornukov: . . . General Kornukov, put General Kamenski on.

General Kamenski:
Kamenski here.

Kornukov: (6:14)
Comrade General, Kornukov, good morning. I am reporting the situation. Target 60-65 is over Terpenie Bay tracking 240, 30 km from the State border, the fighter from Sokol is 6 km away. Locked on, orders were given to arm weapons. The target is not responding, to identify, he cannot identify it visually because it is still dark, but he is still locked on.

Kamenski:

We must find out, maybe it is some civilian craft or God knows who.

Kornukov:

What civilian? [*It*] has flown over Kamchatka! It [*came*] from the ocean without identification. I am giving the order to attack if it crosses the State border.

Kamenski:

Go ahead now, I order. . . ?

And at another location—at Smirnykh Air Force Base in central Sakhalin . . .

Lt. Col. Novoseletski: (6:12)

Does he see it on the radar or not?

Titovnin: (6:13)

He sees it on the screen, he sees it on the screen. He is locked on.

Novoseletski:

He is locked on.

Titovnin:

Locked on. Well, Roger.

Titovnin: (6:14)

Hello.

Lt. Col. Maistrenko:

Maistrenko!

Titovnin:

Maistrenko Comrade Colonel, that is, Titovnin.

Maistrenko: (6:15)
Yes.

Titovnin:
The commander has given orders that if the border is violated—
destroy [*the target*].

Maistrenko:
. . . May [*be*] a passenger [*aircraft*]. All necessary steps must be taken
to identify it.

Titovnin:
Identification measures are being taken, but the pilot cannot see. It's
dark. Even now it's still dark.

Maistrenko:
Well, okay. The task is correct. If there are no lights—it cannot be a
passenger [*aircraft*].

Titovnin:
You confirm the task?

Maistrenko:
Eh?

Titovnin:
You confirm the task?

Maistrenko:
Yes.

Titovnin:
Roger.

And at yet another location—with KAL 007 already having entered Sakhalin airspace and with only five minutes of flying time before being rocketed . . .

Kornukov: (6:21)
Gerasimenko!

Lt. Col. Gerasimenko:
Gerasimenko here.

Kornukov:
Gerasimenko, cut the horseplay at the command post, what is that noise there? I repeat the combat task: fire missiles, fire on target 60-65, destroy target 60-65.

Gerasimenko:
Wilco.

Kornukov:
Comply and get Tarasov here.
Take control of the MiG 23 from Smirnykh, call sign 163, call sign 163, he is behind the target at the moment. Destroy the target!

Gerasimenko:
Task received. Destroy target 60-65 with missile fire, accept control of fighter from Smirnykh.

Kornukov:
Carry out the task, destroy [*it*]!

Gerasimenko:
. . . Comrade General . . . Gone to attack position.

Kornukov: (6:24)
Oh, [*obscenities*], how long [*does it take him*] to go to attack position, he is already getting out into neutral waters. Engage afterburner

immediately. Bring in the MiG 23 as well . . . While you are
wasting time, it will fly right out.
Gerasimenko.

Gerasimenko:
Here.

Kornukov:
So, 23 is going behind, his radar sights are engaged, draw yours off to
the right immediately after the attack. Has he fired or not?

Gerasimenko:
Not yet, not at all.

Kornukov:
Why?

Gerasimenko:
He is closing in, going on the attack. 163 is coming in, observing
both.

Kornukov:
Okay, Roger, understood, so bring in 163 in behind Osipovich to
guarantee destruction.

The Issues:

- Why did the air traffic controller at the Anchorage Control Center, apparently contrary to regulations, treat KAL
  007 (and its accompanying sister flight KAL 015) differ-
  ently than all other flights that night, failing to record its
  already 6.6 miles deviated position from the Cairne Mountain way point?

- Why did the pilots of KAL 007 not think it strange, and not report the fact, that they could no longer communicate with their already too distant Air Traffic Control Center and had to communicate via mediaries (International Flight Service Station over high frequency and KAL Flight 015)?

- Why had not the pilots of KAL 007 been alerted of their increasing deviation by their navigational aids (Inertial Navigation System, VORTAC, Horizontal Situation Indicator)?

- How could the pilots not know that they were off course when the revised Estimated Time of Arrival (ETA) required them to view the very console (INS) that showed the aircraft's deviated position?

- Why was KAL 007 not warned by the RC-135 in its vicinity off Kamchatka which could have communicated through emergency frequency transmission? Why did not the RC-135 warn Air Traffic Control Center at Anchorage of KAL 007's entry into the buffer zone?

- Why did Air Force radar personnel at Cape Newenham and Cape Romanzoff not warn— as they were required to—Anchorage Air Traffic Control Center, or any other unit, of the straying Jumbo Jet?

- Why had the Air Force (The Regional Operational Control Center at Elmendorf Air Force Base in Anchorage), as it has admitted, destroy within 24 to 30 hours after the shoot down (Pentagon Spokesman Michael Burch[196]) the radar tapes it possessed of KAL 007's flight, when the whole world knew within three[197] to ten hours of the shoot-down that a major aviation disaster had occurred, and when it was customary in other incidents of this nature to impound the tapes for detailed analysis and for use in probable future litigation?[198]

- Why was the effective investigation in progress—conducted by National Transportation Safety Board (NTSB) Anchorage station chief, James Michelangelo—preempted (the very first occurrence) by Washington based NTSB home office under orders from the State Department which itself did not, as originally announced, investigate the disaster[199], but rather referred the investigation to the

---

[196] KAL 007: The Coverup, David Pearson, Summit Books, 1987, page 309.

[197] Three hours after the shoot-down was 10 a.m. at Kimpo Airport in Seoul, and the end of the 12-hour fuel supply that KAL 007 was given at Anchorage, Alaska.

[198] See discussion of this issue in Pearson's book, pp. 308-309.

[199] "Normally when an airliner crashes, responsibility for the inquiry falls to the National Transportation Safety Board, which has the technical expertise to assess what happened. Although the downing of Flight 007 cannot be classified as a routine aviation disaster, the N.T.S.B. office in Anchorage was notified that the plane was missing just three hours after it had plunged into the Sea of Japan and immediately began to look into the matter. Shortly after that, it was told to forward to its headquarters in Washington all the material—originals and copies—it had gathered. From there, the information was sent to the State Department. James Michelangelo, chief of the N.T.S.B.'s Anchorage office, was told by headquarters that the board was off the case and that the State Department would handle the investigation. Eighteen months after the airliner was shot down, when asked if the State Department had ever conducted such an inquiry, a high-level State Department official replied,

politically and investigatively ineffective United Nations International Civil Aviation Organization? (The ICAO has no subpoena powers and, according to its mandate, can analyze only material presented to it by its constituent "interested" members. ICAO's final reports are reflections of the politically expedient rather than of an independent investigative determination).

Resistance comes in all forms!

'How is the State Department going to investigate?'" David Corn in *The Nation* magazine, Aug. 17/Aug 24 1985 as quoted by Robert W. Lee in *The New American*, Aug. 29, 1988, Pg. 36

APPENDIX E

Last Moment Comparisons

Unique to our generation is the awful ability to hear the last words of a man, from whom we are removed in time and space, about to die. In every age, soldiers overhear their comrades' last words. Wardens, chaplains and other select personages often hear the last testaments of prisoners about to be executed. But in our generation, the black box— or the component of it called the Cockpit Voice Recorder (CVR)— allows us the privileged and horrific ability to hear the voices of people in the process of being overtaken by death.

US Air Flight 427

September 8, 1994—Pittsburgh, Pennsylvania

Flight 427, for reasons still unknown, has turned over onto its back and in another 16 seconds will hit the ground.

Copilot:
Oh, shit.

Captain:
Hang on. What the hell is this?

Cabin:
[*Sound of stick shaker vibrations indicating imminent stall; sound of altitude alert.*]

Captain:
What the . . .

Copilot:
Oh . . .

Captain:
Oh God, Oh God . . .

Approach:
USAir.

Captain:
Four twenty-seven, emergency!

Copilot:
[Screams.]

Captain:
Pull.

Copilot:
Oh . . .

Captain:
Pull . . . pull . . .

Copilot:
God . . .

Captain:
[*Screams.*]

Copilot:
No . . .

End of tape.[200]

Yukla 27

September 22, 1995—Elmendorf Air Force Base, Alaska

Immediately upon takeoff, Yukla 27, an Air Force Boeing 707 configured as a radar E-3A, took several Canadian geese in engines one and two, disintegrating fan blades. All 24 aboard were lost in the ensuing crash.

Cabin:
Yukla Two Seven heavy's [*indicating large or wide-bodied plane*] coming back around for an emergency return. Lower the nose. Lower the nose.

Tower:
Two Seven heavy, roger.

Captain:
Goin' down.

Copilot:
Oh my God.

Captain:
Oh shit.

Copilot:
Okay, give it all you got, give it all you got. Two Seven heavy, emergency . . .

---

[200] All transcripts in this appendix, except that of KAL-007, are taken from The Black Box, Malcom MacPherson (ed.) (Quill William Morrow, New York: 1998)

Tower:
Roll the crash [*equipment*] roll the crash—
Copilot:
[*Over public address system*] Crash [*landing*]!

Captain:
We're going in. We're going down.

End of tape.

Atlantic Southeast Airlines Flight 529

August 21, 1995—Carrolton, Georgia

21 minutes into its flight, Flight 29's left engine has fallen apart or exploded. Parts of the propeller blades are wedged against the wing and the front part of the cowling is destroyed. The captain and seven passengers will die. The copilot will survive with burns over 80% of his body.

Captain:
[*To copilot*] Help me. Help me hold it. Help me hold it. Help me hold it.

Cabin:
[*Vibrating sound of the stick shaker starts warning of stall.*]

Copilot:
Amy, I love you.

Cabin:
[*Sound of grunting; sound of impact.*]

End of tape.

*   *   *

The transcripts of real-life tragedies as they happen are presented to us in this generation through the marvel known as the Cockpit Voice Recorder, a 2 1/2 pound orange (rather than black) box containing a 30 minute magnetic loop—always recording the previous 30 minutes at any point in an aircraft's flight (CVRs of new commercial aircraft contain two hours of self-erasing solid-state recorders). CVRs have been required by federal law in passenger aircraft since 1966. Only one CVR has yet to be recovered from the ocean floor—that of an Alitalia jet shot down off the coast of Libya, most probably by Libyan interceptors.

Only one CVR that was recovered contains no last moments and no last words—KAL 007's. This incongruity with the reality of the way things ought to happen has been previously explored, but here it ought be noted that an anomaly has occurred comparable with other unique anomalies associated with the case of KAL 007—such as KAL 007's "crash" being the only one in which not a single body or suitcase has been found floating on the surface of the sea, or that of KAL 007's "devastating" crash disgorging only debris from the upper passenger cabin portion of the aircraft and nothing from the lower cargo section.

Comparisons of CVR transcripts of actual air emergencies are invaluable tools for understanding what the pilots of KAL 007 could have done, and indeed did do, to ensure the survival of their aircraft and safety of its passengers. These comparisons also provide us with a scenario of what could have happened to KAL 007 if its pilots had been less skillful and/or less able to work together in bringing their airplane to a safe water ditching.

Firstly, the 1993 ICAO report examined damage done to the aircraft—but none of the areas of damage, not all put together, can account for the sudden termination of its flight. The report would conclude that "all four engines must still have been functioning normally. The flight engineer also twice stated that the engines were normal. This suggested that the infrared guidance missile had not homed directly onto an engine."[201] But this "normal" working of engines

---

[201] ICAO report, 1993, pg. 55, section 2.16.10.

strengthened the indications, as did the Digital Flight Data Recorder information and the cockpit electronic transmits, that the electrical systems were also working normally.

Furthermore, aside from the damage to the tail portions from the Anab missile detonated 50 meters from the aircraft (a missile containing 20 kg high explosive warhead designed to produce 1,400 steel fragments, each of three to 18 grams.[202]), there was no evidence of damage to the jumbo jet anywhere except "holes with a total area of 1.75 square feet."[203]

This meant that structural damage itself to the fuselage of this aircraft could not account for the supposed disintegration of the aircraft or its "crash." The 11 second lapse between fragment impact and the warning alert of escaping air furthermore indicated, supported by CVR transcripts (pilot now speaking through his oxygen mask) that the plane could not have gone out of control because of pilot disorientation due to oxygen insufficiency.

This then left the malfunctioning of the control surfaces due to the missile impact itself (tail section) or due to loss or damage of hydraulic systems as the only apparently supportable explanation for both the supposed loss of pilot control and supposed loss of aircraft ability—required to explain a cataclysmic (and undocumented) crash.

The damage to the tail section involved damage to, and almost immediate unraveling of, the cable that connected the left inboard elevator to the right outboard elevator,[204] which resulted in the ensuing upward pitch of the aircraft. The CVR reveals this to be the immediate concern of the pilots.

Captain: (6:26:24)
Altitude is going up. Altitude is going up!

Captain: (6:26:25)
Speed brake is coming out.

---

[202] ibid., pg. 39, section 1.16.22.

[203] ibid., pg. 54, section 2.16.4.

[204] ibid., pg. 54, section 2.16.2

Copilot: (6:26:26)
What? What?

Captain: (6:26:29)
Check it out.

Copilot: (6:26:33)
I am not able to drop altitude—now unable.

Captain: (6:26:38)
Altitude is going up.

Captain: (6:26:40)
This is not working. This is not working . . . [205]

The effect of the above mechanical damage would be evaluated by ICAO investigators in the light of failures in KAL 007's hydraulic systems as an aircraft's hydraulic systems are designed to maintain control of its moveable surfaces during its flight ensuring stability of the aircraft's three axes.[206]

---

[205] ibid., pg. 13.

[206] These three axes are:

> Lateral axis—conceptually an axis through the side of the plane, rotation about which is called "pitch" (determining the positioning of the plane relative to the forward horizon.) The elevators located in the trailing edge of the horizontal tail section control this axis.
>
> Longitudinal axis—conceptually an axis through the length of the plane, rotation about which is called "roll" (determining the positioning of the plane relative to the lateral horizon). The ailerons located in the trailing edge of the wings control this axis.
>
> Vertical axis—conceptually an axis through the plane, top to bottom, rotation about which is called "yaw" (determining the positioning of the plane relative to its flight path). The rudder located in the trailing edge of the vertical tail controls this axis.

Based on the triple axes Digital Flight Recorder charts of KAL 007's post-hit flight (charts which also provide other information such as altitude and acceleration changes), as well as investigators' conclusions from these charts which bear on hydraulic functioning, we can recreate the in-cockpit drama from the time of missile impact relating that to aircraft functioning—until the end of the black box recording—a span of one minute and thirteen seconds. For our purposes, we need only deal with the first 50 seconds of the post-hit flight.

Here, then, is the reconstruction. The missile detonates. Captain Chung calls out, "What was that?" The plane has suddenly increased its forward acceleration and begins to both pitch its nose upward and to ascend in altitude. The copilot responds, "What?" The aircraft, now a few seconds after missile impact, begins roll to the right. This motion will eventually end after 40 seconds, with the right wing down 50 degrees. Sixty degrees is considered dangerous. "The aircraft rolled very slightly right wing down."[207] The captain calls out, "Reduce throttles." The copilot responds, "What?" The rate of aircraft acceleration decreases slightly, but the aircraft is still rising. Yaw, which had begun immediately upon missile detonation, diminishes slightly. Chun, who had been turning the wheel (to control aircraft roll) with large movements, at eight seconds after detonation has been able to reduce his movements to small corrections. But at eight seconds after detonation, Chun says, "Altitude is going up. Altitude is going up." The control column, which ought to have moved forward automatically to put the nose down (the plane was on autopilot), does not move forward. This failure indicates that hydraulic system number three, which operates the autopilot Actuator A control system of the elevators was damaged or out. Hydraulic system number three also provided one half of the power for the inboard left and outboard right elevator surfaces. KAL 007 was flying with one half power to its elevator surfaces.

Captain: (6:26:38)
Altitude is going up.

---

[207] ibid., pg. 54, section 2.16.

Captain: (6:26:40)
This is not working. This is not working.

The autopilot is either tripped or switched off by Captain Chun—presumably to move the column forward himself. The column does move sharply forward but the aircraft does not respond and continues its upward arc.

Captain: (6:26:41)
Manually.

Copilot: (6:26:42)
Cannot do manually.

This failure of the elevator to respond to manual control of the column indicates that there were failures in hydraulic systems one and two. These systems also controlled the yaw dampers, which explain why oscillating, yawing motions were experienced immediately upon missile detonation.

CVR transcripts of actual air emergencies provide us with an incident that fleshes out for us what it might have been like in the cockpit of KAL 007. There are striking similarities in the cases of KAL 007 and this incident, but KAL 007 might indeed have been in a more enviable position.

The incident unfolds with United Airlines Flight 232, a DC-10 piloted by 58-year-old Captain Al Haynes on July 19, 1989, on a flight from Denver, Colorado, to Chicago, Illinois. The aircraft was at 37,000 feet altitude, about 2,000 feet higher than KAL 007 when it was hit, when the jet experienced an explosion of its number two engine, located in its tail. Engine and fan blade parts severed and destroyed all three of its hydraulic systems (Flight 007 retained full operational capability of one of its hydraulic systems—number four. There is no indication of damage to hydraulic system number four. "With the wing flaps up, lateral control of the Boeing 747 aircraft was achieved with the inboard ailerons and the five outer spoiler segments on each wing. When the only hydraulic power available was system number four, control was reduced to the right inboard aileron and the innermost of the spoiler segments on each side." ICAO, 1993, pg. 54, section 2.16.4.)

Like Flight 007, Flight 232 was able to execute turns in only one direction—to its right. Like Flight 007, Flight 232 had sufficient engine power (engines one and three in the wings were operating normally). Oxygen was likewise sufficient and there was no evidence, aside from the tail section, of significant structural damage.

Common problems had to be faced—stability with minimal rudder and elevator power, maneuvering turns (232 was able to do this by increasing and decreasing power alternately to its two remaining engines), ensuring stability in banks, however slight, lowering the landing gear, either by gravity or by cranking (Flight 007's crew were possibly presented with this problem as a ground landing on Sakhalin Island might have been contemplated at first), and precise calculations for the dumping of fuel, guaranteeing enough left over to ensure arriving at the desired destination but not enough to cause an explosion if the landing were "hard." Quite like Flight 007's final flight path, Captain Haynes and his flight crew brought his DC-10 down in large spirals, seeking to land at Sioux City, Iowa. The DC-10 had traveled more than 18 miles after descending from 37,000 feet to 33,000 feet with zero hydraulics.

Upon touchdown at runway 22 at Sioux City Airport, the right wing tip made contact with the runway, subsequently breaking the right main landing gear. The airliner skidded off the runway and turned upside down in a corn field. Most of the right wing and tail section were broken off. Of the 296 passengers and crew aboard, 185 survived, including Captain Haynes.

For the purposes of comparison with Flight 007, only those portions of the transcript, which illuminate the process, and experience of flying without hydraulic power are here presented. This will amply illustrate and support the contention that Flight 007 certainly could have been flown a short distance on at least one-quarter hydraulic power if a DC-10 could be flown a longer[208] distance on no hydraulic power whatsoever.

SAM[209]:
United Two thirty-two, is all hydraulic quantity gone?

Flight Engineer:
Yes, all hydraulic quantity is gone.

Copilot:
Level off.

Approach:
United Two thirty-two heavy, souls on board and fuel remaining?

Copilot:
Souls on board and fuel remaining. We have thirty-seven six [*on fuel*].

Flight Engineer:
We've got thirty-seven four on fuel.

Approach:
Roger . . .

Copilot:
What's the hydraulic quantity?

Flight Engineer:
Down to zero.

---

[208] General Kornukov ordered the shooting down of KAL 007 as it was leaving Soviet airspace and about to enter international waters. Flight 007's flight after missile impact would have been about 14 to 16 miles. See chart in Appendix G.

[209] United Airlines Systems Aircraft Maintenance representative.

Copilot:
On all of them?

Flight Engineer:
[*On*] all of them.

Haynes:
Quantity, quantity is gone?

Flight Engineer:
Yeah, all of the quantity is gone. All pressure is [*gone*].

Haynes:
[*Did*] you get hold of SAM?

Flight Engineer:
Yeah, I've talked to him.

Haynes:
What's he saying?

Flight Engineer:
He's not telling me anything.

Haynes:
We're not going to make the runway, fellas. We're going to have to
    ditch this son of a bitch and hope for the best.

Cabin:
[*Sound of three knocks.*]

Haynes:
Unlock the damn door.

Copilot:
Unlock it.

Haynes:
We've lost . . . no hydraulics. We have no hydraulic fluid. That's part of our main problem . . .

Jumpseat Captain:
[*Returning to cockpit*] Okay, both your inboard ailerons are sticking up. That's as far as I can tell. I don't know . . .

Haynes:
Well, that's because we're steering, we're turning maximum turn right now.

Jumpseat Captain:
Tell me. Yell what you want and I'll help you.

Haynes:
Right throttle. Close one, put two up. What we need is elevator control. And I don't know how to get it.

Jumpseat Captain:
Okay, ah . . .

Flight Engineer:
[*To Dispatch*] Roger, we need any help we can get from SAM, as far as what to do with this. We don't have anything. We don't [*know*] what to do. We're having a hard time controlling it. We're descending. We're down to seventeen thousand feet. We have . . . ah, hardly any control whatsoever . . .

Haynes:
You want full aileron and full elevator. No, no, no, no, no, not yet. Wait a minute. Wait till it levels off. Now go.

Flight Engineer:

[*To Dispatch*] Well, we can't make Chicago. We're going to have to land somewhere out here, probably a field.

Haynes:

How're they doing on the evacuation [*preparations*]?

Jumpseat Captain:

They're putting things away, but they're not in any big hurry . . .

SAM:

United Two thirty-two, we [*understand that you*] have to land [*at*] the nearest airport, the nearest airport. Ah, I'm tryin' to find out where you've lost all three hydraulic systems.

Haynes:

Well, they'd better hurry. We're going to have to ditch, I think.

Jumpseat Captain:

Get this thing down. We're in trouble . . .

Flight Engineer:

[*To SAM*] That is affirmative. We have lost all three hydraulic systems. We have no quantity and no pressure on any hydraulic system . . .

Haynes:

[*To Sioux City Approach*] Sir, we have no hydraulic fluid, which means we have no elevator control, almost none, and very little aileron control. I have serious doubts about making the airport. Have you got someplace near there, ah, that we might be able to ditch? Unless we get control of this airplane we're going to put it down wherever it happens to be.

SAM:

Ah, United Two thirty-two, you have lost all manual flight-control systems?

Flight Engineer:

That's apparently true . . .

Approach:

United Two thirty-two heavy, can you hold that present heading, sir?

Haynes:

This is Sioux City, Iowa. That's where we're headed . . .

SAM:

He has no control. He's using that kind of sink rate, I believe. This is what he's doing. He's got his hands full for sure.

Haynes:

Okay, thank you. [*To Jumpseat Captain*] You're a little more . . . Let's see if you can make a left turn.

Jumpseat Captain:

Left turn. All right. Your speed is what? I'm worried about [*it*]. I don't want to stall you . . .

Fitch²¹⁰:

You lost the engine, huh?

Haynes:

Yeah, well, yeah. It blew. We couldn't do anything about it. We shut it down.

Fitch:

Yeah.

---

²¹⁰ A training pilot for United riding in First Class.

Flight Engineer:

[*To SAM*] Go ahead with any help you can give us.

SAM:

United Two Thirty-two, understand that you have one and three engines operating. You have absolutely no hydraulic power. You
have no control over the aircraft. Is that correct? . . .

Haynes:

Come on back, come on back, come on back . . . As soon as that [*is*]
vertical, go for it, go for it. Watch that vertical speed the second
it starts to move. Come back, come back, come back. Go for it. If
we can get this under control elevator-side we can work on steering later.

Cabin:

[Laughter.] . . .

Haynes:

Anybody have any ideas about [*what to do about the landing gear*]? He
[*the flight engineer*] is talking to SAM.

Fitch:

Yeah, he's talking to SAM. I'm gonna alternate-gear you. Maybe that
will help you. [*But*] if there is no [*hydraulic*] fluid, I don't know
how the outboard ailerons are going to help you.

Haynes:

How do we get [*landing*] gear down?

Fitch:

Well, they can free fall. The only thing is, we alternate the gear. We
got the [*landing gear*] doors down?

Haynes:

Yep.

Copilot:
We're gonna have trouble stopping, too.

Haynes:
Oh, yeah. We don't have any brakes.

Copilot:
No brakes?

Haynes:
Well, we have some brakes [*but not much*] . . .

[*To Approach*] We're just passing it [*the highway*] right now. We're gonna try for the air[port]. [*To Fitch*] Is that the runway right there? [*To Approach*] We have the runway in sight. We have the runway in sight. We'll be with you shortly. Thanks a lot for your help.

Fitch:
Bring it on down . . . Ease 'er down.

Copilot:
Oh, baby.

Fitch:
Ease her down.

Haynes:
Tell 'em [*the passengers*] that we're just two minutes from landing.

Approach:
United Two Thirty-two heavy, the wind's currently three six zero at one one three sixty at eleven. You're cleared to land on any runway . . .

Haynes:

[*Laughs.*] Roger. [*Laughs.*] You want to be particular and make it a runway, huh?

Flight Engineer:

[*On public-address system to passengers*] Two minutes. Two minutes . . .

Fitch:

Yeah, I can see the runway, but I got to keep control on ya.

Copilot:

Pull it off a little.

Haynes:

See if you can get us a left turn.

Copilot:

Left turn just a hair, Al.

Haynes:

[*To Approach*] Okay, we're all three talking at once. Say it [*the wind*] again one more time.

Approach:

Zero one zero at one one, and there is a runway that's closed, sir, that could probably work to the south. It runs northeast to southwest.

Haynes:

We're pretty well lined up on this one here . . .

Fitch:

I'll pull the spoilers [*speed brakes*] on the touch[*down*].

Haynes:

Get the brakes on with me.

Approach:

United Two Thirty-two heavy, roger, sir. That's a closed runway, sir, that'll work, sir. We're gettin' the equipment off the runway. They'll line up for that one.

Haynes:

How long is it?

Approach:

Sixty-six hundred feet, six thousand six hundred. Equipment's comin' off.

Haynes:

[*To crew*] Pull the power back. That's right. Pull the left one [*throttle*] back.

Copilot:

Pull the left one back.

Approach:

At the end of the runway it's just a wide-open field.

Cockpit unidentified voice:

Left throttle, left, left, left, left . . .

Cockpit unidentified voice:

God!

Cabin:

[*Sound of impact.*]

APPENDIX F

Correspondence

Correspondence from Helms to Yeltsin

December 5, 1991
His Excellency
Boris Yeltsin
The President of the Russian Republic
The Kremlin
Moscow, USSR

HAND DELIVERED

Dear Mr. President:

The status of the thousands and thousands of American servicemen who were held by Soviet and other Communist forces, and who were never repatriated after every major war this century, is of grave concern to the American people.

As you may be aware, the United States Senate recently created a Select Committee on POW/MIA Affairs. The entire POW/MIA issue has been given impetus by extensive media coverage of photographs purporting to show U. S. Servicemen alive and still held in captivity in Southeast Asia.

The recent publication of previously highly classified U. S. government documents has heightened the concerns of the American people. One of these documents, a memorandum circulated at the highest levels of the Supreme Headquarters of the Allied European Forces, stated that three weeks after the conclusion of World War II, the Stalin government still held 20,000 American soldiers. These men were being held in Nazi prison camps in Eastern Germany when the camps were overrun by what were then Red Army forces. These Americans were never repatriated.

Similarly, previously classified U. S. Government documents stated that 954 U. S. Soldiers were not repatriated by Communist forces after the Korean War. Other evidence exists that all U. S. Personnel in the custody of Communist forces in Southeast Asia were not repatriated.

Please use your good offices, and your influence with the new Minister of Defense, Mr. Shaposhnikov, and the new head of the MSB, Mr. Bakatin, to facilitate the release of any GRU or MSB intelligence reports, files or information that may ease the pain for thousands of American families who have never learned the fate of their loved ones.

The United States must resolve this sensitive issue to restore its honor. In working with you towards this goal, we hope to forge a closer, democratic relationship with Russia. Your assistance will be remembered by all Americans.

Sincerely,
 cc: The President, The White House, Washington, D.C. U.S.A. 20500

December 10, 1991

His Excellency
Boris Yeltsin
The President of the Russian Republic

The Kremlin
Moscow, USSR

Dear Mr. President:

One of the greatest tragedies of the Cold War was the shoot-down of the Korean Airlines flight KAL-007 by the Armed Forces of what was then the Soviet Union on September 1, 1983.

This event had an element of a personal catastrophe for me, since I was on the parallel flight that night on KAL-015, which departed Anchorage, Alaska about fifteen minutes after KAL-007. Both flights stopped in Anchorage for refueling. I shall never forget mingling with the doomed passengers of KAL-007 in the transit lounge, including two sweet young girls who waved goodby [sic] to me when they were called to return to their fatal flight.

The KAL-007 tragedy was one of the most tense incidents of the entire Cold War. However, now that relations between our two nations have improved substantially, I believe that it is time to resolve the mysteries surrounding this event. Clearing the air on this issue could help further to improve relations.

Accordingly, I respectfully request that the government of the Russian Republic gain access to the files of the former KGB and of the Minstery [sic] of Defense in order to resolve the attached questions. I hope that you will personally intervene with the relevant authorities of the former Soviet Union in order to provide answers to these questions.

The American people, indeed, the families of all passengers on KAL-007, will be deeply grateful for your efforts.

Sincerely,

JESSE HELMS:
QUESTIONS ON KOREAN AIRLINES FLIGHT KAL-007

I. KAL-007 Landing

1. Please provide deposition or accounts from eye witnesses who saw KAL-007's landing.
2. Please provide the geographical coordinates of the location of where KAL-007 landed.

II. Eye Witness Accounts from Soviet Military Radar Tracking Stations

1. Please provide depositions or accounts from eye witnesses from Soviet military tracking station who saw the track of KAL-007's descent.
2. Please provide the exact locations of these military radar tracking stations, and a map showing their disposition.
3. What was the ground and air tracking range of these military tracking stations?
4. How far away from the KAL-007 landing site were these tracking stations and their command posts?

III. Soviet and Japanese Radio Transmissions Related to KAL-007

1. Please provide transcripts of all available Soviet civil and military radio transmissions related to the entire flight of KAL-007.

2. Please provide transcripts of all available Soviet intercepts of non-Soviet radio transmissions related to the flight of KAL-007.

IV. KAL-007 Passengers and Crew

1. From Soviet reports on the incident, please provide:
    a) A list of the names of any living passengers and crew members removed from the airplane;
    b) A list of missing passengers and crew;
    c) A list of dead passengers and crew
    d) A list and explanation of what happened to the bodies of any dead passengers and crew;
    e) A list of items of luggage and other items removed from the plane;
    f) A list and description of the disposition of the luggage recovered and any other recovered items, and where such material is now kept;
    g) A description and disposition of any other recovered cargo.

2. How many KAL-007 family members and crew are being held in Soviet camps?

3. Please provide a detailed list of the camps containing live passengers and crew, together with a map showing their location.

V. Soviet Search and Rescue Efforts

1. Please provide a copy of the reports of all Soviet search and rescue operations, and the military and KGB "after action" reports.

VI. Information on Congressman Larry McDonald

1. Please provide detailed information on the fate of U. S. Congressman Larry McDonald.

Correspondence from Wendy R. Sherman to Senator Graham

FEB 21 1996

Dear Senator Graham:

Thank you for forwarding the correspondence from Mr. Bertram Schlossberg regarding the fate of the passengers of Korean Airlines Flight 007 which was shot down by the Soviet Union on August 31, 1983. The contention that planes passengers and crew survived the shootdown and are probably alive today in the former Soviet Union is not a new one. This allegation along with other conspiracy theories surrounding the KAL 007 tragedy continues to percolate. No substantive evidence has been produced to support any one of them.

The International Civil Aviation Organization (ICAO), a United Nations specialized agency, located in Montreal, Canada, was charged with the initial investigation of the KAL 007 incident in 1983. In 1992 the Russian government released to ICAO the Cockpit Voice Recorder and the Digital Flight Data Recorder which they had recovered from the wreckage and which ICAO then read out and analyzed. The Russian government also made available to ICAO tapes and transcripts containing air-ground communications between the U.S.S.R. interceptor aircraft and their command centers, and ground-ground communications between the U.S.S.R. Air Defense command centers. With this information ICAO was able to issue a final report on the KAL 007 incident in 1993.

In its final investigative report, ICAO concluded that KAL 007 was hit by at least one of two air-to-air missiles fired from a U.S.S.R. SU-15 interceptor aircraft. There was substantial damage to the aircraft which affected its controllability and the plane was destroyed upon impact with the sea. The wreckage of KAL 007 was located at 46 3332N 141 1941E 17 nautical miles north of Moneron Island in international waters at about 174 m depth over an area of about 60 x 60 m. The report concluded that there were no survivors. The U.S. government accepted the findings of the ICAO report, and believes that no credible evidence has been produced by anyone that contradicts or undermines its conclusions.

I hope this information is helpful to you. If you have any other questions, please do not hesitate to contact us again.

Sincerely,

Wendy R. Sherman
Assistant Secretary
Legislative Affairs
Enclosure:
Correspondence returned.

APPENDIX G

Charts, Maps & Illustrations

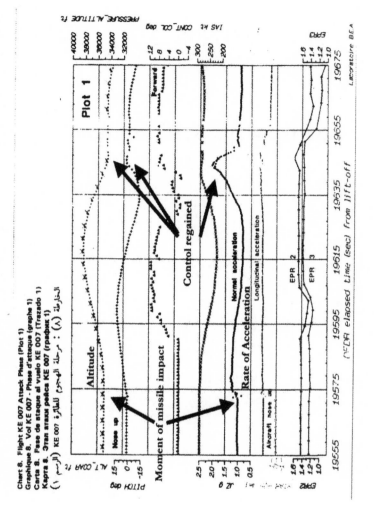

Digital Flight Data Recorder Chart (DFDR)

Note change in altitude and rate of acceleration at moment of missile impact. Note the regaining of control—Altitude: Dive is stopped and gradual descent begins. Pitch: Nose has been brought up as pilot breaks dive. Rate of Acceleration: Sharp rate of acceleration has been stopped and deceleration begins as KAL 007 levels out at pre-impact altitude. Aircraft exhibits major parameters of control as it begins graduated descent.

After Action Report Map
From Commander, Combatant Force Seventh Fleet

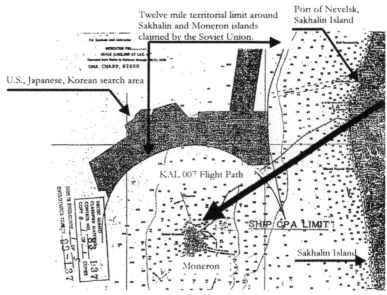

*After Action Report Map
From Commander, Combatant Force Seventh Fleet*

This computer-aged picture shows Congressman Larry MacDonald as he might have appeared in the mid 1990s. Note the faint scar from the left of his nose to the edge of his lip. MacDonald was identified by the wardens of the prison north of Temir-Tau, Kazakhstan, through this picture, as the probable prisoner brought there from Karaganda. (See pg. 122)

APPENDIX H

Avraham Shifrin—
Israeli Investigator of the KAL 007 Tragedy

By Eleonora Poltinnikov-Shifrin
(© 2000 Eleonora Poltinnikov-Shifrin, used by permission)

Avraham Shifrin, one of the most non-conformist figures in the literary and social-political world of Israel.

He was born in 1923 in Minsk, Belorussia into the family of rank and file technical intelligentsia, and was raised in Moscow. His engineer father Isaak was arrested for telling a joke when Avraham was fourteen, which overnight turned a light-hearted lad into an enemy of the hypocritical and ruthless Soviet system. He swore to avenge his father (and eventually he did). Since that point his whole life became one long detective story.

At the out-break of World War II, Avraham was drafted to the Red army and sent to the front line to serve in a penal battalion, along with many other sons of "enemies of the people." They were all sent into battle with no weapons and were told, "Your weapons are in the hands of the enemy—go and take them". Some were lucky and remained alive. Those who were wounded were supposed, according to the Soviet law, to be transferred into a regular unit. Avraham was among them, but after he recovered he was sent back to the penal battalion and again into battle with no weapons. Realizing that the authorities were simply trying to do away with those who were perceived as a natural enemy, Avraham decided he would not let them dispose of him. On the way to the hospital he threw away his papers and changed his identity. Thus he got lost to the KGB and started making a regular front-line career. He finished the war as a decorated officer with clear papers which allowed him to proceed building his civilian career as well. He was looking for an opportunity to harm the Soviet power. Eventually he reached the position of a chief legal adviser of the Ministry of Weapons, which gave him such an opportunity. He became probably one of the first volunteer spies for the USA in the Soviet Union and was finally arrested in 1953 (already after Stalin's death) when a Soviet mole in the CIA reported that highly sensitive information kept coming from the very top of the arms production system. Avraham was initially sentenced to be shot; the sentence was then commuted to 25 years of strict labor camps plus another 10 of exile and curtailment of legal rights. In the camps he participated in *seven* escape attempts, therefore, served most of the time in the strictest and harshest prisons and camps.

Even prior to his arrest, Avraham became active in gathering and disseminating information about the newly established Jewish State which became the land of his dream. In 1948 when hundreds of Moscow Jews, at the suggestion of Golda Meir, Israel's first ambassador in the USSR, compiled lists of volunteers to go to fight for the independence of the young Jewish state, Avraham could not participate in this activity simply because he was working away from Moscow at the moment. So, he miraculously avoided arrest when all the participants were arrested and sent to the camps where most of them perished. But when he was finally arrested his indictment and sentence emphasized his Zionist activities.

While in the camps, he translated Leon Uris's *Exodus*, a book that later played a crucial role in the development of the Jewish consciousness in the Soviet Jews. Also in the camps he became interested in and started studying esoteric sciences and religious philosophy eventually becoming an expert in the field. It was in the camps that he wrote his first work on the subject, "The Universe And Mankind"— a short but capacious essay. Due to the changes in the political situation in the USSR, he finally served only 10 years in the camps and 4 in exile. But as a combined result of the war wounds, interrogation torture and numerous frostbites while cutting timber in the camps, Shifrin lost his right leg. Later in Israel, Shifrin wrote a book describing his camp experience, *The Fourth Dimension*, which was published in Germany by "Possev" in 1973. It was later translated into Hebrew and German and published respectively by "Maoz" in Israel and by "Stephanus-Verlag" in Germany.

Following a period of active participation in the underground Zionist movement in the U.S.S.R. in the course of which he organized Jewish underground in Odessa and established secret ties with Israel, Shifrin arrived in Israel in August, 1970. Here, in spite of the vigorous opposition of the establishment, he developed the struggle for the freedom of exit to Israel for Soviet Jewry, organized numerous demonstrations and hunger strikes to support this political demand and attract world public opinion to the plight of Soviet Jewry. The first major "Free Soviet Jewry!" demonstration in Israel took place in December 1970; it was a hunger strike organized by Avraham Shifrin to support the Leningrad Jews who were on trial for an attempt to highjack a plane to fly to Israel. The unexpected success of that demonstration made the then Prime Minister Golda Meir say: "The Soviet Jews have shown us how they should be fought for!" That emotional exclamation did not change much in the governmental line vis-a-vis the Soviet Union, and fighting for the release of the Soviet Jewry still meant being a persona non-grata in Israel. Nevertheless, Avraham succeeded in organizing a number of other big and noisy demonstrations, one of the most successful being the mass hunger strike of over 200 former Soviet Jews in the summer of 1973 at the time of President Nixon's visit to Moscow. It resulted in the immediate release of numerous *refuseniks* that kept arriving straight from Moscow during all the days of the hunger strike.

In September of 1970 Avraham met the 'Singing Rabbi", Rabbi Shlomo Carlebach ZT"L and introduced him to the Soviet Jewry plight. Rav Carlebach's first trip to Moscow on *Simhas Toira* of 1970 was conceived and organized by Avraham and they remained close friends ever since.

Upon his arrival in the West Avraham realized just to which extent this same "capitalist West" was tainted with Soviet agents, infiltrated with the Soviet propaganda and poisoned with Marxist ideology. Avraham started fighting against this. Unfortunately, the situation at home, in Israel, wasn't any better; therefore he had to fight against his own Israeli establishment.

One of the first large-scale operations that Avraham organized in the West was the undercover sending of Jewish and anti-Soviet literature to the USSR. For that purpose a used van was purchased (with the help of a Jewish millionaire from London) and modified in such a way that there now were hidden places to house books all around the vehicle. Simultaneously, the van could contain up to 1200 books. It was so well done that for five consecutive years the van would travel twice a year to the U.S.S.R. loaded with books and was never caught at the border until one day an overly meticulous border-guard simply drilled the bottom of the car and saw paper chips running down . . .

In 1973 Avraham Shifrin appeared before the U.S. Senate Committee for the Judiciary at the first special Hearings on Soviet labor camps. His two-day testimony was then published as a Senate document, translated into numerous languages and spread throughout the world. A map depicting 120 Soviet camps and prisons that Avraham compiled for the Hearings was hung in the National Museum in Washington, D.C. and even caused a diplomatic scandal when the Soviets demanded that the map be immediately removed. In subsequent years Avraham was many more times invited to testify before various Senate and House Hearings that dealt with the USSR's industry, the KGB, the USA-USSR trade, communist anti-Semitism and other related subjects. In 1973 Avraham received the award "The Anticommunist of the Year" along with John Barron.

In 1974 Avraham married Eleonora Poltinnikova, an activist of first the human-rights and then the Zionist movement, who arrived from Novosibirsk in 1972. His work was conducted with her active participation ever since. They were married by Rav Carlebach with participation of Rav I.M. Lau and the young Rav Kook.

In 1974 Avraham established a Research Center for the Soviet Prisons, Psychiatric Prisons and Forced-Labor Concentration Camps. He ran it till the end of his life and in its framework, practically on his own (with the help of only his wife) conducted a mammoth re-search work dealing with various aspects of the Soviet prison-camp system. Over twenty research works on the subject were published and distributed throughout the years . . .

In 1978 a 30-minute documentary movie-film "Prisonland" was released and sent to the Belgrade international conference on human rights. It depicted Soviet forced-labor camps and prisons and was based on footage secretly filmed in the U.S.S.R. and smuggled out. Former inmates presently residing in Israel were commenting. For ten years that followed this film remained the only documentary film on the subject in the world. It was screened on major TV channels of 25 countries. In Denmark it was even shown twice within one month, the second time after being chosen the best program of the month. In the Parliaments of Great Britain, Canada and Australia there were special shows organized for the politicians.

In 1979 a special study was published on the Soviet women's camps and specifically camps for women with children. It caused a tremendous sensation in the world—mainly due to the very stupid reaction of the Soviets who labeled Avraham a slanderer, "second Goebels", Number One enemy etc., and declared that there had never been any camps for women with children in the USSR. The sensa-tion lasted for an entire two months and subsided after the USSR's Supreme Soviet had announced . . . a general amnesty for women with children up to 7 years of age and reduced the term to a half for women with children up to 12 years. Those were the children who "had never been in the camps", as the Soviets insisted.

In 1980, as a very special gift for the Moscow Olympic Games, *The First Guidebook to the U.S.S.R. Camps, Prisons and Psychiatric Pris-ons* was published. It contained 2300 addresses, maps, pictures, eye-witness testimonies. The cover of the book copied that of the Soviet official guidebook, which enabled many tourists to take it safely through the border and even find some camps and prisons (some of them in the center of Moscow). The book also caused a sensation and re-ceived the "Book of the Year" award in Europe in 1980.

Throughout the years Avraham conducted very intensive lecture work in the world and was considered one of the world's leading experts on the Soviet penitentiary system and the KGB . . .

For the last nine years of his life Avraham conducted an independent investigation of the fate of KAL 007 flight –the ill-starred South Korean airliner that was hit by the Soviet rockets over Sakhalin Island in 1983 and disappeared after that. The Soviets claimed for years that the plane had crashed in an unknown place and everybody on board perished. Avraham managed to prove that the plane had water-landed, the passengers were removed from it alive and taken to secret camps, while the plane, stripped of its electronics, was towed away to a deep-water place, sunk and blasted on the bottom of the sea. Moreover, it was established in course of the investigation that the American side had known of that monstrosity all along from the very beginning, but the information was hushed up in order not to interfere with the relaxation policy between the two superpowers . . .

Avraham had two children in Israel by Eleonora, Miriam-Ester (23) and Izhak-Gabriel (16). Ten days prior to Avraham's death his grandson was born, Shlomo-Dov-Yair, at whose *brith* Avraham was the *sandak*.

For years Avraham suffered from terrible, excruciating pains in his legs—both the one that was and the one that wasn't, but this never stopped him from being active, from doing what he thought was the right thing to do.

On March 5 1998, Avraham Shifrin died of a heart attack. He is laid to rest on the Mount of Olives ancient cemetery overlooking the Temple Mount.

APPENDIX I

A Tribute

(And An Exemplification Of The Role Of Hate, Fear And Spite As
"Sufficient Cause" In Personal And Public Oppression.)

Commentators quest for the possible reasons for the downing, cover-up and cover-ups of the cover-ups related to flight KAL 007 but sometimes overlook the role of illogical but powerful personal factors that are "sufficient cause" in themselves.

For example, Commander of Sokol Air Force Base, General Kornukov's insistence to his superior commander of the Far East Military District Air Force, General Kamenski, that KAL 007 had to be shot down before it reached international waters is considered by some as motivated by clear knowledge of (and conventional guidelines of response based upon) the Soviet Union's failure to prevent the deep penetration of a previous Korean Airlines flight over Russian territory in 1978 (Murmansk).

But could not that fateful insistence and decision be motivated by a man having been "bested", having become frustrated and thwarted? Are not the irrational, "ephemeral", but powerful emotions we know as pride, resentment, revenge and spite important motivating factors in fateful political and military decisions as they are so often in personal ones?[216] Aren't these the dynamics that are revealed as Kornukov's "cool" is unraveled through his insistence to his superior that KAL 007 be shot down and to his haranguing of his subordinates as he becomes aware that KAL 007 has survived?

---

[216] Cannot much of recent Middle East history be understood only by appreciation of the personality and character traits of Yasser Arafat and Saddam Hussein?

Kamenski: (6:14)

We must find out, maybe it is some civilian craft or God knows who.

Kornukov:

What civilian? [*It*] has flown over Kamchatka! It [*came*] from the ocean without identification. I am giving the order to attack if it crosses the State border . . .

Kornukov (to Gerasimenko): (6:24)

Oh, [*obscenities*], how long [does it take him] to go to attack position, he is already getting out into neutral waters. Engage afterburner immediately. Bring in the MiG 23 as well . . . While you are wasting time, it will fly right out . . .

Kornukov (to Gerasimenko): (6:29)

. . . I do not understand the result, why is the target flying? Missiles were fired. Why is the target flying? [*obscenities*] Well, what is happening?

Gerasimenko:

Yes.

Kornukov:

Well, I am asking, give the order to the Controller, what is wrong with you there? Have you lost your tongues?

Gerasimenko:

Comrade General, I gave the order to the Chief of Staff, the Chief of Staff to the Controller, and the Controller is giving the order to . . .

Kornukov: (6:30)

Well, how long does it take for this information to get through, well, what, [*you*] cannot ask the results of firing the missiles, where, what, did [*he*] not understand or what?

*   *   *

The following is a tribute by Eleonora Politinnikov-Shifrin to her family. But, it also, of necessity, unveils before us the irrational hate-fueled, spite-filled personal essence of evil in the harangues, harassments and devious and effective persecutions emanating from a great and corrupt political system as it crushes its individuals. It illustrates this point—having penetrated finally to what is evil and irrational, we need seek no further for explanation. None will be found.

A Monument to My Family

By Eleonora Poltinnikov-Shifrin
(© 1994, Eleonora Poltinnikov-Shifrin, used by permission)

On June 22,1989, a ceremony took place in Netanya, Israel, to mark the dedication of a new street to my father, blessed be his memory, Dr. Izhak Ben-Khanan (Poltinnikov), a physician, a scientist, a veteran of WW II and an *aliya* activist, who died on July 1, 1986.

The decision to name a street in his honor was taken by the municipality of Netanya following the application of the Union of Veterans of War Against Nazism which was supported by the Union of Disabled Fighters of WW II as well as by the Eye Institute of the Tel-Hashomer Hospital in Israel. This decision stands as the last military honors Israel paid to three soldiers who fell in the battle for *aliya*: to my parents and sister. The names of my mother and sister— Dr. Irma Bernstein and Dr. Victoria Poltinnikov—have been engraved on my father's tombstone, as their remains are buried in Novosibirsk, USSR. The monument is common for the three, as common was their heroism and tragedy and common are the honors.

We were among the first families in Novosibirsk who decided to apply for exit permit in 1971 when there was no exit at all from there. The tactical question was debated then among the potential "applicants" in the Siberian city: whether to apply right there and "break the wall" or first move to one of the Baltic Republics or to Chernovtsy where the Jews were already getting exit permits. In our family the decision was taken without any disagreement: to apply on the spot. Probably, that was foolhardy, taking into account my father's position. He was a recently retired colonel, after 30 years of service in the medical corps of the Soviet Army. He was chief ophthalmologist of the Siberian Military District, head of the eye department of the district military hospital, and elected chairman of Eye Diseases Department of the Medical Institute in Novosibirsk (which position was immediately cancelled). He was recognized as the best eye surgeon in the Asian part of the country to whom high rank officers from all Siberian districts would try to go to be treated and operated on.

Probably, it would have been wiser to hide far away from that fame. But my parents never in their lives sought easy ways, and so the question of the right for exit was immediately phrased by them in most precise and clear terms: "it is not only our personal exit that matters but the right for exit in general; this right is legal, and if the authorities are trying to deprive us of this right, we have to struggle for it—here and now."

"If I am not for myself, then who is? But if I am only for myself, then what am I for? And if not now, then when?" This Jewish wisdom had never been taught to my completely assimilated parents, but it was in their Jewish blood, in their Jewish character.

Our application for exit caused rabid anger among the authorities. "You will rot here but never leave"—declared Col. Gorbunov, then head of the OVIR to my father. The repression followed immediately. At the general meeting, called in the hospital where my father had started to work upon his retirement from the military, the young nurses and physicians were shouting: "It is a pity Hitler did not finish with all of you! If I just had a pistol I would myself shoot you, traitor!" They were shouting all this to a man who had spent all the years of WW II at the front line as a field surgeon, was three times wounded and many times decorated for valor.

A similar meeting was gathered at the Research Institute of Tuberculosis where my sister Victoria worked as a junior researcher and from which she was immediately fired. At the meeting Victoria clearly expressed the essence of the Zionist idea and heard in response: "If she at least had a millionaire aunt in that filthy Israel but this way it turns out she is a traitor for ideological reasons—such people should be just killed!"

My father was reduced to the ranks and deprived of all the privileges and pension earned during the thirty years of military service, and then also fired from his job.

At that time I was already in Israel. At the moment of our application for exit permit, proceedings against me were taken by the KGB in connection with the distribution of the underground literature, I was interrogated in the KGB and threatened with a camp term; therefore, my mother, who had before saved me from poliomyelitis, tuberculosis of the backbone, and rheumocarditis and who was now afraid that a camp would mean a death sentence for me, arranged my fictitious marriage to a man with a visa to Israel. In November, 1972, I left for Israel taking with me my 84-year-old grandfather whose exit permit was granted immediately upon the application and who was told in the OVIR office that the rest of the family would follow soon after. The reason they were so eager to send my grandfather away was his desirable apartment which was wanted by others.

Immediately upon our departure my parents and sister were denied exit permits with the fashionable explanation: "inexpedient." They applied again and were once again denied—this time on the grounds they "had no close relatives in Israel." In December, 1972, my mother and sister were arrested (along with dozens of Jews from various cities) during the attempt to hand their petition to the Supreme Soviet of the U.S.S.R. in Moscow. Most of those arrested were sentenced to fifteen days of administrative detention. Unlike the others, my mother and sister were sent back to Novosibirsk by a freight train and there sentenced to half a year prison term. My mother had suffered three heart attacks by then and was diabetic, while my sister had active tuberculosis.

At this point I started meeting with Israeli and Western diplomats and other political figures trying to organize a campaign for my family. In February 1973 at the invitation of the American Jewish organizations I came to the USA where the mass media very soon picked up my family's plight. In the meanwhile, my mother suffered a high blood pressure crisis in prison and Victoria had a bad attack of tuberculosis. Apparently scared of the public campaign that started in the USA, the Soviets released them after three months. But the repression did not cease. All three of them were summoned to the militia and were commanded to find themselves jobs immediately, otherwise they would be prosecuted for parasitism. My mother, who was officially registered as an invalid because of her heart condition, and my father who was no longer considered retired were included. However, in the city health department they were officially notified that there are clear instructions not to employ the Poltinnikovs in any capacity in any medical institution of the city. I managed to organize their employment as consultants in the American hospitals with fees transferred to them through official channels, but in Novosibirsk they were told, "this is not to be accepted as work—you do not participate in the construction of socialism." At the same time the local newspaper in Novosibirsk started publishing articles accusing my father of having made experiments on human beings (in spite of the fact that up until the KGB ban he continued to be invited to all city clinics to perform the most subtle and complicated operations).

During that period, in all their telephone conversations with me and with the American Jewish activists (I have the tapes of those conversations) my parents and sister would endlessly repeat, "do not concentrate on us, our situation is hard, but we are still strong, we shall endure, others need help more urgently."

In March, 1973, my grandfather (who was temporarily staying with relatives in Switzerland) died—having spent his last ten days by the telephone repeating over and over, "They will call and say they are allowed to leave." He was not sick, he simply died of anguish, of separation. My mother demanded permission to attend the funeral— and was denied. After this my father put into a box all the blood-earned decorations and mailed them to the Supreme Soviet of the

USSR, with an accompanying wire: "I need no decorations from murderers."

Following this act of protest all three of them began a hunger strike—an endless hunger strike—in a public building housing the Long Distance Calling Center, demanding that exit permit should be given to them immediately. I learned of their hunger strike upon arrival in Switzerland for the funeral. Having buried my grandfather, I flew to London and there started a hunger strike in front of the Soviet embassy. Previously I called the head of the Novosibirsk district department of the Ministry of the Interior, Gen. Slanetsky and offered a compromise: I would quit my campaign in the West, if they would let my family out. The reply was clear and laconic: "You can croak there at your hunger strike—your parents and sister will rot here, they will never leave."

My mother fell unconscious on the third day of the hunger strike. Instead of the ordered ambulance the KGB came and said cynically: "there would be no medical help until all three ceased their hunger strike." While supporting my mother with injections and pills, my father and Victoria continued their hunger strike. Following ten days of my hunger strike in London and my fictitious husband M. Yampolsky's hunger strike in Washington all the American and European media were full of publications and programs about the plight of the Poltinnikovs. European parliament members as well as American Senators and Congressmen were sending individual and collective letters to Moscow. The American State Department sent an official request to the Soviet government to release my family. This was only the second time during the first three years of the Soviet Jewry struggle, that the American State Department had taken this action. It seemed that now they would be released—and we stopped our hunger strike. A month later they received another refusal—this time it was motivated by some classified information my father had had access to many years before.

In 1974 they declared another hunger strike—in support of Alexander Feldman who was arrested in Kiev. This way it continued until the beginning of 1975, when my mother suffered her fourth heart attack. She was treated for it at home because in the emergency room of the hospital she, a specialist in cardiology, managed to notice that, with her blood pressure falling down at a catastrophic rate, they intended to inject her with a medicine that lowers blood pressure.

Mail would not reach them. Their telephone was disconnected from the very beginning, while to the Long Distance Calling Center they were invited for the wrong time, they would waste days and nights sleeplessly. My father was hit by a car while walking along a sidewalk (nobody knows if it was deliberate—there was no investigation) after which he also suffered a heart attack. Our dog, a dedicated guard and friend that had lived in the family for many years, was stolen. And then—the first time after all those hard years—In one of the last telephone conversation an outcry sounded: "We are being killed by attrition, we have no energy left, save us!"

In March 1975, their last letters came to me and to our friends in the West. They wrote that they had no more energy for an active struggle and that they intended to use the last means at their disposal, i.e. a complete boycott of the Soviet authorities on all issues except for one—getting their exit visas. "Do not expect any more letters from us. We shall either get our exit permit or die here."—they wrote.

They reckoned that being so widely known in the West—they had over three hundred regular Jewish as well as Christian correspondents in the USA, Canada, and Europe—their situation would stir up the world. They didn't realize that the world remembers about you as long as you remind the world of your existence. American supporters failed to understand the seriousness of Poltinnikov's threats. Other refusenicks would write, shout, remind the world about themselves constantly. But the Poltinnikovs barricaded the entrance door from the inside and stopped both going out or letting anyone in. The only exception was tourists from the West. But most tourists would go to the Soviet Union having with them just a list of refusenicks, and very few would think of getting in touch with me prior to their visit. Their Moscow contacts usually told them: "Do not go to the Poltinnikovs, do not waste your time, they don't want to see anyone anyway." And none of those who took the liberty to speak on behalf of the *aliya* movement bothered to travel to Novosibirsk and find out at least if the Poltinnikovs were alive at all. Rare tourists would visit them at their own risk and left shocked and upset, having left whatever they had with them, because what they saw was incredible. They discovered that my parents and sister used to lower a basket on a rope from their fourth floor balcony with money (if and when they had it) or their belongings (as long as they had what to offer for exchange) and ask the passers by to bring some food instead. Some would bring it, others would take the money and disappear.

They were simply starving; there were periods when they ate half an ounce of bread a day; they would eat potato peelings and alike, throwing away practically nothing. In spite of all this they were studying Hebrew, listening to Western radio stations, my father was writing poems in Hebrew. The walls of their apartment were covered with maps of Israel and numerous postcards with pictures of Israel. The windows were curtained tightly with blankets because my mother was sure they were being watched through those windows. Perhaps it just seemed so to my mother who was becoming paranoid—nobody will ever know.

During all that period I managed to gain the support of numerous American Senators and Congressmen. All the lists of the refusenicks submitted to the Soviet authorities contained the names of the Poltinnikovs. Official requests and inquiries from the U.S. Senate and Congress continued to go to Novosibirsk without an end. Finally, the Soviets gave in. In February 1979, I was notified from Novosibirsk that my family had been granted exit permit. But the information came from strangers who also added that my family refused to walk out of their apartment to pick up the exit permit because they believed it was a trap. As I found out later, prolonged starvation and isolation caused the loss of reason in my mother and sister. They insisted that the talk about the exit permit was nothing but provocation aimed at luring them out of the apartment in order to kill them. My father who disagreed with them was forcefully kept in the apartment.

Our Christian friend Alice Ford, of the Jerusalem group of Pentecostal Zionists, who had visited my family before, went there again at my request and begged them to go with her, under her escort. She told them, "Whatever will happen to you will happen to me too." The U.S. Embassy in Moscow sent a cable wherein official guaranties of their safety were offered up until they cross the borders. Nothing helped. Then my father determined to make a last and extreme step. He broke out of the apartment determined to arrive in Israel and thus prove to his wife and daughter that the way was indeed safe. Felix Kochubievsky, a Novosibirsk refusenick helped him arrange all the documents and leave. My father arrived in Israel on May 31,1979, hardly able to stand on his feet. He was 5'6" inches tall and weighed only 98 pounds.

My father's last hope proved futile—my mother and sister refused to accept the letters and pictures we sent from Israel. Instead, they went on a hunger strike demanding exit permits. We addressed the authorities in Novosibirsk from here, while Felix Kochubievsky, with my father's power of attorney, did the same there. We demanded that the two sick women should be either hospitalized in a psychiatric clinic or sent out to Israel by force. But the authorities answered cynically, "They were insane when they wanted to leave. Now they don't want to leave which means they are quite sane."

On August 5, 1979, my mother died of starvation. Following this, and under the pressure of F. Kochubievsky, Victoria finally was hospitalized but in a regular hospital that had neither facilities nor stuff to care for mentally ill patients. She was left unattended and nobody even noticed when she walked out the next day. She came back to the apartment, hammered a nail into a wall, tied her hands behind her back and hanged herself.

In spite of two heart attacks my father suffered after that, he managed to pull himself together and began working. His research in the field of immunology of eye burns was so innovative that a separate laboratory was created for his research at the Eye Institute of Tel-Hashomer Hospital. His discovery in the field of eye burns treatment was rewarded with the Goldshleger special prize. He also developed methods for treatment of cataracts that, according to Prof. M. Belkin, the Head of the Eye Department of Tel-Hashomer hospital, are truly revolutionary.

A month after open-heart surgery, on July 1, 1986 my father, Dr. Izhak Ben-Khanan, died.

This August, 1994, 15 years have passed since the destruction of my family. Time does not cure wounded souls—it is as hard for me as before to talk about this. But being the only surviving member of the family, the duty falls on me to tell our terrible story, for those Jews who leave the former U.S.S.R. today with comparative ease must know how it all started, how the history of our fight and our Exodus was being written with blood, how we were going through our "wilderness" striving for our Israel.

HELP SPREAD THE STORY OF KAL 007 AND ITS SURVIVORS!

Additional copies of this book may be obtained directly from Xlibris Corp.
Call 1-888-795-4274 (Toll free within North America). fax: 1-215-923-4685 email: *info@xlibris.com*

436 Walnut St. 11 Fl.
Philadelphia, PA 19106

Rescue 007: The Untold Story of KAL 007 and Its Survivors is also available through *www.amazon.com, www.barnsandnoble.com* and *www.borders.com.*

See the authors Web page at: *www.xlibris.com*

Special pricing available for bookstores, libraries and resellers. Contact Xlibris Corp.

For inquiries or offers of information, contact:

The International Committee For the Rescue of KAL007 Survivors
P.O. Box 43
South Windsor, CT 06024
USA
or
P.O. Box 44143
Pisgat Zeev
Jerusalem Israel